Advance Praise

"This book is essential reading for any teacher committed to making their part of the world a better place, for their students and for themselves. It speaks to teachers and teacher educators in ways that are clear, direct, illustrative, and compelling. It draws on teachers' voices, ideas, and projects consistently and respectfully. Moreover, it focuses on what teachers *can* do within their classrooms, schools, and districts, recognizing the incredible diversity among students, teachers, and their contexts."

—**Mollie Blackburn**, editor of *Adventurous Thinking: Students' Rights to Read and Write*

"Cathy Fleischer and Antero Garcia believe in teachers. They also believe in advocacy. In this thoughtfully constructed, informative text, they provide excellent reasons why teachers can and should be advocates for students and educational practices that respect learners and learning. Importantly, they surround the stories shared by teachers and teacher educators with useful frameworks that invite educators to realize advocacy in their classrooms. Quite simply, they make advocacy seem not just possible, but also absolutely necessary."

—**Bob Fecho**, Professor & Program Director,
English Education, Teachers College Columbia University

"Educational 'reform' has been under the control of politicians, billionaires, corporations… everyone but teachers and teacher educators. This volume assembles an impressive roster of educators who understand classrooms and kids, and who know what needs to be done to make their learning more relevant and the lives of educators themselves more satisfying. It's time that the people running things start listening to them, and this book is a great place to start."

—**Peter Smagorinsky**, Distinguished Research Professor, The University of Georgia

"*Everyday Advocacy* is a usable, practical guide to help teachers and teacher educators think about approaches to extend their critical thinking about traditional pedagogies to include advocacy for all children, particularly historically marginalized students. This can be an active teaching method, used to impact change for and with students, employing storying through technology and other community and extended spaces to address needs."

—**Tonya B. Perry**, Ph.D., Professor and Executive Director of
GEAR UP Alabama and Red Mountain Writing Project

"Cathy Fleischer and Antero Garcia's *Everyday Advocacy* provides fresh insight into how teacher educators might help candidates advocate for literacy learning beyond the classroom. By modeling reflective practice in local schools and communities within today's contentious social and political climate, *Everyday Advocacy* builds upon decades of teacher research and knowledge from leaders in the field. This volume is timely and a welcome addition to conversations about teaching in our current environment of societal redefinition and change."

—**Ebony Elizabeth Thomas**, Associate Professor, University of Pennsylvania, and author of
The Dark Fantastic: Race and the Imagination from Harry Potter to The Hunger Games

"With a thoughtful, welcoming, and encouraging approach, Cathy Fleischer and Antero Garcia have written a book with (and for) teachers that show us how to advocate for change across the spectrum of the educational landscape. Each chapter represents a slice of everyday advocacy that is smart, safe, savvy, and sustainable. Become a powerful advocate for change, on your own terms, focused on the change you would most like to see."

—**Andy Schoenborn**, author of *Creating Confident Writers: For High School, College, and Life*

"*Everyday Advocacy* is a must-have for educators everywhere. Antero Garcia and Cathy Fleischer invite all of us into the world of advocacy work. They help us expand the definition of what it means to advocate, and they give us many ways to join in the work of changing the narrative of literacy education. I can't imagine a more important time for this book."

—**Franki Sibberson**, educator, author, NCTE Past President

everyday
advocacy

everyday advocacy

TEACHERS WHO CHANGE the LITERACY NARRATIVE

CATHY FLEISCHER
and **ANTERO GARCIA**

Foreword by Elyse Eidman-Aadahl

W. W. NORTON & COMPANY
Independent Publishers Since 1923

For information about permission to reproduce selections from this book, write to Permissions, W. W. Norton & Company, Inc., 500 Fifth Avenue, New York, NY 10110

For information about special discounts for bulk purchases, please contact W. W. Norton Special Sales at specialsales@wwnorton.com or 800-233-4830

Manufacturing by Sheridan Books
Book design by Joe Lops
Production manager: Katelyn MacKenzie

Library of Congress Cataloging-in-Publication Data

Names: Fleischer, Cathy, author. | Garcia, Antero, author.
Title: Everyday advocacy : teachers who change the literacy
narrative / Cathy Fleischer and Antero Garcia.
Description: First edition. | New York : W. W. Norton & Company, 2021. |
Series: Norton books in education | Includes bibliographical references and index.
Identifiers: LCCN 2020022625 | ISBN 9780393714371 (paperback) |
ISBN 9780393714388 (epub)
Subjects: LCSH: Educational change—United States. | Educational leadership—United States. |
Teachers—Political activity—United States. | Educators—Political activity—United States. |
Teachers—Training of—United States. | Teacher participation in administration—United States.
Classification: LCC LA217.2 .F58 2021 | DDC 370.973—dc23
LC record available at https://lccn.loc.gov/2020022625

W. W. Norton & Company, Inc., 500 Fifth Avenue, New York, N.Y. 10110
www.wwnorton.com

W. W. Norton & Company Ltd., 15 Carlisle Street, London W1D 3BS

1 2 3 4 5 6 7 8 9 0

Dedicated to the memory of Kent Williamson,
whose legendary devotion to teachers and
advocacy is at the center of it all

Contents

Foreword

I distinctly remember my first visit to Congress as part of the National Writing Project's annual Teachers' Day on The Hill. A teacher and teacher educator at the time, I hadn't really imagined myself trodding the halls of Congress, riding the little subway train in the basement of the Capitol Building to get from the House of Representatives to the Senate and back, passing the little underground signs for the Senate dry cleaners or the Congressional barbershop.

But there I was, wearing a brand new suit and carrying a briefcase filled with "leave-behinds" and student work.

My first visit was in the surprisingly small office of my local representative. As my writing project colleagues and I sat nervously in the waiting room, we could hear the receptionist over the intercom room say with excitement, "The teachers are here!" Another voice, one that we later learned came from the legislative aide, replied with equal eagerness, "Great. Show them to the meeting room."

That first visit so many years ago was a revelation: *these congressional staff were as eager to see us as we were to meet with them.* And in the meeting that followed, they asked question after question about what was actually happening in our classrooms, about what could make a positive difference for young people, about what we saw as the unintended consequences of policies in place. Mostly, they wanted to hear stories of how policy affected the real work of teaching and learning told from people they considered a trusted source: actual teachers.

I learned many lessons that day that have informed my current work in the National Writing Project, lessons that are beautifully conveyed in *Everyday Advocacy.* I learned that something as seemingly distant as a trip to Washington, DC to visit Congress was, at base, a simple human process of planning and organizing that was well within reach of any teacher. I learned that "policy-makers" were people who might be as ready to listen as I was to speak. And I learned to be prepared with solid information and a focused message, yes, but more importantly, I needed to come prepared with a powerful *story*.

The Story Is the Story

When I was a teacher, I was rarely encouraged to think of my work as *advocacy*, a word that sounded to some as "too political" for what teachers might do on a daily basis. Sitting in that congressional office, of course, I couldn't avoid taking up the word: I was unquestionably engaged in advocacy. But even there I was being educated; introduced to a different vision of advocacy, one closer to the message of this book, through my conversations with policy makers and the stories they told.

In one office a senior aide shared how enrolling her son in summer writing camp helped her understand what we meant about reducing emphasis on testing writing to make space and time for "real writing." She explained how the teachers leading the camp had made it a point to explain its philosophy and to invite parents to visit and observe. "I got it in a different way," she said. "They, and my son, helped me see that creative work and academic work aren't necessarily in competition." In another office, a young staffer talked about how her favorite writing teacher often shared with the class the dilemmas of teaching. We helped her connect those stories to the larger story of American education. And in one case, a senator meeting with us talked about how an elementary teacher he knew helped him understand the importance of professional development through a story about the faculty at his old elementary school. He remarked: "She was the most credible expert I've ever heard about education."

My colleagues and I saw that although we were the ones sitting in the offices, that official "advocacy visit" was preceded by a long line of stories, explanations, and small public teaching moments that paved our way. I doubt that any of the teachers who had done that important initial work saw themselves as doing anything other than what teachers do, but their everyday advocacy proved to be an essential part of creating the conversation that can lead to change.

When Teachers Tell the Stories

Cathy Fleischer and Antero Garcia, referring to stories such as those I heard from the policy-makers, note: "Stories like these contribute to a public narrative that gradually takes on a kind of truth in the world, a truth that is mostly narrated by outsiders to the world of classrooms and teachers and students."

What would it take to change that? How do we invite more teachers to contribute to the public narrative about education, about youth and their potential, about their families and communities? What would it take for us to be the authors of our own profession?

As longtime members of the NWP, Fleischer and Garcia know the power and importance of learning to tell our own stories, both for how those stories shape the larger narrative and for how those stories shape our inner lives as educators. This book, and its important collection of stories by educators engaged in everyday advocacy and teacher educators exploring everyday advocacy with both their pre-service and practicing teachers, aims to be part of the change. *Everyday Advocacy* clarifies how *advocacy knowledge* can be, at its core, a form of *pedagogical knowledge* at work in the wider world. Through the stories of educators not so different from us, we learn how our work in the world can be smart, safe, savvy, and sustainable.

The educators collected here are doing their part to build a strong and positive narrative for education. Our part is for us as educators to use our "outside voices" and claim a place in the public sphere.

Even now, as public satisfaction with experts, institutions, and each other plummets to an all-time low (July 2019), the public still generally trusts teachers and principals, still gives positive marks to their local schools, and increasingly shares teachers' concerns over the adequacy of funding (PDK, 2019). Majorities say they would even support teachers in decisions to strike for better pay and working conditions. While polls such as the PDK Poll of the Public's Attitudes Toward the Public Schools portray teacher morale at a low point and frustration at a high point, it is important to know that we, as teachers, teacher educators, and local administrators, are still perhaps our communities' most trusted and direct source of information and perspectives on education.

That trust is a precious and powerful commodity—and a good place to begin our journey with *Everyday Advocacy*.

Elyse Eidman-Aadahl
Executive Director, National Writing Project

References

PDK (September 2019). Frustration in the Schools: Teachers Speak Out on Pay, Funding, and Feeling Valued. *PDK Poll of the Public's Attitudes Toward the Public Schools*, A supplement to *Kappan* magazine,

Rainie, Lee and Andrew Perrin (July 22, 2019). *Key Findings About Americans' Declining Trust in Government and Each Other,* Pew Research Center.

Acknowledgments

Writing this book has been a journey of learning and a testament to the remarkable commitment of many teachers, teacher leaders, and teacher educators who have contributed to our growing understandings. We begin by thanking those educators whose inspiring chapters fill this book, as well as those whose words and ideas are sprinkled throughout. We also want to recognize those who have helped us deepen our awareness about how to advocate in complicated times, in particular, the many teachers who have participated in Everyday Advocacy workshops and whose ideas shine through on every page of the book. We are grateful to all of you for your patience in helping us grow in our understanding, and we hope we have represented your work well.

We are indebted to the incredible team of teacher educators who have helped create and revise the Everyday Advocacy website that figures centrally in these pages. Jenna Fournel was Cathy's thought partner in the original creation of that site and her commitment to and knowledge of this kind of work is foundational to every word on these pages; Amber Jensen with her design eye helped make the site come alive in its early stages; and Sarah Hochstetler, Amber Jensen, Jennifer Dail, Christine Dawson, and Rae Oviatt have thoughtfully and critically rethought and updated the site. We also thank the NCTE ELATE Commission on Everyday Advocacy for their input and advice.

We appreciate the kind words of Elyse Eidmann-Aadahl who wrote a beautiful foreword to this book, one that captures her own story of advocacy and sets the stage for the stories of others who follow. As Executive Director of the National Writing Project, Elyse has long supported this work.

We are grateful to the team at Norton Professional Books for their belief in this project and their thoughtful responses to our drafts. From the moment Carol Collins approached us to see if we might be interested in writing about this work, we were wowed by her understanding of its importance and her commitment to bringing these ideas out in the world. Jamie Vincent, Mariah Eppes, and others at Norton helped bring this book to life.

Our families and friends have exhibited support and understanding, as well as time and space, so that we could immerse ourselves in the kinds of thinking, writing, revising, and editing that any text needs—but especially one collaboratively written by authors who live three time zones and 2000 miles apart. (Thank goodness for Zoom and Google Docs!) Cathy thanks, in particular, her husband Andy Buchsbaum, an environmental advocate and self-described "recovering attorney," for inspiring her interest (some might say obsession!) in advocacy, as well as the many lessons taught during dinner conversations and the careful and critical reading of much of this book. Antero is grateful for the patience of his work from home coworkers: Ally, Joey, Stella, Olive, and Grant; their harmonies of barks, cries, and competing Zoom meeting discussions served as the soundtrack during the completion of this manuscript.

Introduction

We believe in teachers. We believe in their power to inspire, challenge, support, and care for the students with whom they work—day-in and day-out, in often challenging circumstances, and with intelligence and grace. Teachers, we know, are contemporary superheroes, and we believe they should be honored as such, each and every day.

But we live in a world where that's not always the case. Too often teachers become easy targets for criticism or sitcom satires, their deep knowledge largely ignored in both local conversation and state and national policymaking.

We believe that has to change. And we've written this book to help teachers, teacher leaders, and teacher educators learn concrete steps to change the public narrative about teachers, literacy education, and the ways to best educate students. We've written this book to help teachers find their voices, honor their own stories, and translate their experiences in ways that will help the public understand what they do, why they do it, and what that means for students and their learning. We call this Everyday Advocacy, the everyday steps teachers can do—and are doing—to help others understand differently.

We are two university-based teacher educators, both former high school teachers, who are lucky enough to collaborate with teachers who have been committed to advocacy for many years. What brought us to this work? Here are our advocacy origin stories:

Cathy Fleischer

For the past two decades I have been thinking and writing about teacher advocacy, beginning with the book *Teachers Organizing for Change: Making Literacy Everyone's Business.* For that book, I interviewed community organizers from various disciplines and teachers from multiple grade levels, exploring the ways that teachers do indeed practice (sometimes without realizing) many of the tenets of community organizing in their outreach to parents, families, and colleagues. Since then, I have read widely in the field of community organizing theory and practice, taught courses and led workshops in advocacy for teachers, and eventually began a collaboration with Jenna Fournel, former Communications Director for NCTE. Jenna has experience with issues of organizing, particularly in her previous work at FrameWorks Institute, a group devoted to helping nonprofit groups learn strategies for framing their issues so that they promote better communication. Together, Jenna and I created the Everyday Advocacy website (www.everydayadvocacy.org), which was designed to help literacy teachers learn how to become advocates. (Many of the ideas in this book draw upon material found on the Everyday Advocacy website.) More recently, I have received a National Writing Project grant to support Everyday Advocacy Ambassadors as they help teachers and teacher leaders spread the word about advocacy.

Antero Garcia

My work as a classroom teacher in Los Angeles often focused on "big A" advocacy that connected classroom life with my students to activism and social justice. However, through work focused on forms of play and youth participatory action research (YPAR), I have explored the possibilities of teachers and students sharing expertise and guiding school and pedagogical practices through actions that mirror Cathy's articulation of *everyday* advocacy. At the same time, along with Cindy O'Donnell-Allen, I have written about "culturally proactive" approaches to literacy instruction in the book *Pose, Wobble, Flow.* Working to actively support teachers and teacher educators in taking charge and leading the charge toward literacy instruction and equity, Cathy and I have been in conversation about the possibilities of centering advocacy in the ways we prepare and support educators today.

In the past few years, we—Cathy and Antero—began working together to promote the idea of everyday advocacy, most directly through a series of SLAM (Studies in Literacy and Multimedia) videos. These videos, in which I interviewed Cathy and a variety of teachers who have been practicing everyday advocacy, gave teachers an opportunity to share with a larger community their own advocacy work and the changes that have resulted from that work.

What to Expect in This Book

This is a book designed to help teacher leaders and teacher educators—those who work with teachers in many roles—introduce preservice and practicing teachers to the world of advocacy. Whether you are a curriculum director, a methods instructor, a National Writing Project teacher consultant, a lead teacher, or a teacher in a Professional Learning Community, we believe that you have a place in helping teachers learn the strategies and skills of advocating for the best literacy practices we know work for students.

Here's what to expect: In the first part of the book, we introduce the importance of advocacy for teachers—for their own self-preservation, for the kinds of curriculum and pedagogy that support literacy, and, ultimately, for the students they teach. We believe that advocacy is something that can be taught, and we believe that teacher leaders and educators have an obligation to find ways to integrate advocacy knowledge into their teaching. We introduce concepts of everyday advocacy, outlining specific strategies for advocacy, and offering suggestions for how to include advocacy moments in your own pedagogies for undergraduate courses and continuing professional development for teachers. In doing so, we hope to provide both a solid base of resources and to pique your interest in learning more.

One way to use this book to inspire the preservice and practicing teachers with whom you work is to share some of the specifics of everyday advocacy offered in Chapters 1 and 2. A next step would be to share with them the stories of teachers who are practicing advocacy in diverse and successful ways, which you'll see in Part II. We hope that as new and practicing teachers read these case studies, which were written by teachers who are immersed in this kind of work and which are bounded by the particular contexts in which the studies occurred, they might see commonalities, raise questions, and consider how the experiences of these teachers might be reflected in their own context. Rather than serving as perfect models, destined for imitation, these stories are offered as a way to elicit conversation and to lead to new ways of thinking.

We offer the same approach in Part III, this time focusing on how other literacy educators—those who teach methods classes, those who lead workshops for teachers, those who work with groups of practicing teachers—are introducing advocacy. As like-minded educators, we hope you see these examples, too, as thoughtful steps toward creating new ways of thinking among the teachers and preservice teachers with whom you work, ways that in turn might impact how you too can help change the public narrative.

We believe this is important work, work that is vital to changing the public narrative about teachers, about teaching literacy, and about students. Teachers can become change agents in a world that is too satisfied with the status quo (or even one that longs for an imagined way of teaching that no longer exists). When teachers learn strategic ways to advocate for themselves and their approaches to teaching, we shift the conversation in ways that give voice to those who are most intimately acquainted with classrooms and students. We invite you to join this movement and help spread the word of everyday advocacy.

everyday advocacy

PART I

What Is Everyday Advocacy?

If you're a teacher or a teacher educator, you know that these are rocky times. Statistics tell us that more teachers than ever—especially teachers with less than five years of experience—are leaving the profession and that enrollment in teacher education programs across the country is rapidly decreasing (Ingersoll, Merrill, Stuckey, & Collins, 2018; King, 2018). Anecdotes from our friends and colleagues who are committed and devoted teachers tell us that their jobs are getting harder and harder as mandated models of teacher assessment, required curricula, pacing guides, and district-wide end-of-course student assessments become the norm. Newspapers, social media, and legislation tell us that respect for and trust in teachers has diminished even as untenable classroom conditions are on the rise and teacher pay, benefits, and basic rights are experiencing a free fall.

This context is the backdrop for this book. We—and many teacher educators we know—care deeply about the issues facing our colleagues and former students who are teaching English language arts in secondary schools. We care deeply about creating and implementing literacy curricula and practices that are based on the most current and inclusive research about the subject of English language arts. And we also care deeply about the students they teach—young people who are deserving of a literacy education that relies on research-based practices in reading and writing. And so, we challenge ourselves every day to think through some complicated questions about our role as literacy educators. How can we best do our job of educating and mentoring new and practicing teachers in times like these? How might we work with teachers to support them as they move into careers that too often recreate practices that we know are not congruent with literacy research and best practices? What can we do differently to help teachers survive and even thrive in such difficult circumstances?

Traditionally, we teacher educators have centered our instruction around the golden rule of teacher preparation: teachers need to be well-versed in both *content knowledge* and *pedagogical knowledge*, that is, "a deep understanding of the critical concepts and principles of their discipline . . ." and the ability "to use discipline-specific practices flexibly to advance the learning of all students . . ." (Council for the Accreditation of Educator Preparation, n.d.) or, as Lee Shulman (1986) named it, *pedagogical content knowledge.* In response to this sensible understanding, teacher educators have designed programs and created curricula that not only introduce and support teachers in becoming knowledgeable in the content of literature, writing, linguistics, and literacy practices, but also emphasize a specialized kind of approach to that content, one that prepares teachers to be more than mere subject matter specialists. In other words, we recognize the intellectual enterprise that underlies *teaching* literature or writing or linguistics or literacy practices. The goal of teacher educators, then, has been to help teachers at multiple points along their journey from preservice to veteran teacher to become well versed in the pedagogical content knowledge of a discipline so they can put into practice the very best of what we know from research and experience. In doing so, students benefit.

Teachers who have been immersed in this approach have learned both the content of their discipline and how to teach their discipline. For many years, that knowledge has been enough. However, the worlds that teachers now occupy are far different from what they were in the past—they're more complicated, more demanding, and, sadly, more accusing. Teachers are judged on how well their students do on standardized tests, tests that too often are based on curricula that are contextless and antithetical to research-based practices. Media portrayals of teachers either applaud the hard-working individualism of the teacher who defies all odds to help students learn or diminish teachers to caricatures who are portrayed as unprepared, unprofessional, and uninterested. You can ask any teacher who steps onto a plane, meets new people at a dinner party, or stands on the sideline of a soccer game: when we reveal that we are teachers, far too often we are told what's wrong with kids today and what's wrong with the way we teach. Teachers, caught between standardized forces and public opinion, are increasingly disheartened and discouraged (Thomas, n.d.; Rich, 2016).

Because the very narrative surrounding teachers and teaching has changed so drastically, we've come to believe that pedagogical content knowledge is just not enough to ensure teachers success in their jobs. Too often these days, the kind of thoughtful, research-based instruction that is at the core of pedagogical content knowledge appears at odds with calls for mandated curricula, standardized approaches to pedagogy, and standardized assessments. Teachers, who at one time were able to rely on their own knowledge base to teach in these research-based ways, now find themselves conflicted: How can they teach young adult literature, choice reading, workshop models, project-based learning, grammar-in-context, etc., when the mandated curriculum suggests otherwise? How can they explain to administrators, parents, community members, and even other teachers, why they want to teach in these research-based ways? And how might they advocate for the systemic changes that are necessary to better reflect the needs and interests of a constantly shifting student body?

What we've seen is a shift not only in the narrative surrounding education, but also in what counts as professionalism for teachers. For many years, teachers who knew their content area and how to teach that content area were respected as the professionals they were. But to be a professional today, teachers need to do far more. Successful educators in this new era need to go beyond the *what* and *how* of teaching literacy; they need also to be confident in their knowledge of *why* they teach in certain ways and, most importantly, *how* they might help others understand their reasons. In a time of critiques and misunderstandings by parents, community members, and legislators, we suggest that teachers learn a host of new strategies: strategies for finding their voice, taking a stand, and changing the narrative surrounding teaching, particularly around teaching literacy. In other words, we need a new golden rule for teacher education, such as: in preparing and supporting teachers, we should focus on content knowledge, pedagogical knowledge, and *advocacy knowledge*.

In this first section, we introduce the idea of advocacy by immersing you in the theories that underlie this approach to change-making, some specific strategies that we have used to help teachers begin to identify themselves as advocates, and examples from teachers who have participated in our workshops. As you read, consider your own role as teacher, teacher leader, or teacher educator. What resonates with you? How might these ideas might help you start thinking through an advocacy lens?

Chapter 1

Introducing Everyday Advocacy

Why It Matters

As educators, we are experts at recognizing the needs of our students. Advocating for our learners is part of what we do naturally. Casual conversations with colleagues in the hallways, on the way to the parking lot, and at extracurricular activities depict our passion for education and our desire for student success. All too often, however, these moments of clarity get lost in the shuffle and never make it past our utopian ideology.

Everyday advocacy is the vehicle that can transport ideas to reality. The "elevator speech," structured research, and practice of attaining allies afford educators the tools necessary to turn a conversation into a foundation for success. As educators, our collective voices hold awesome power. When we follow the methods of everyday advocacy, we portray a succinct message that not only has staying power but opens the doors for action.

—Jeffrey Taylor, middle school teacher

In this book, we invite you to think with us about how to extend what we do as teacher leaders and teacher educators to integrate an advocacy component into our overall teacher education curriculum, our individual classes, and the professional learning experiences we share with practicing teachers.

Jeff eloquently explains how he has come to understand the power of becoming an everyday advocate. "But," we can almost hear you say, "teachers are already overwhelmed and overextended. They have full-time jobs. They don't have the

energy, the bandwidth, the expertise to add one more thing to an overly full plate."
We understand this—we really do—but we want to reiterate that we need to do
something about the education crisis in which we find ourselves so that teachers
will be able to remain in the profession and to teach in the research-based ways
that support true literacy. For teachers to reclaim their roles as professionals,
changes must be made. If we literacy educators begin to rethink our practice—
how we work with preservice and practicing teachers, how we initiate them into
a new kind of professionalism—if we can help teachers see advocacy as part of
the mindset of what they do as a part of their jobs, we can help kickstart a cycle
of change. Such change has the potential to remake the narrative that surrounds
literacy education.

How do we help more teachers begin to think as advocates, to do as teacher/
school librarian Beth Shaum explains, "to put on my advocacy cap"? Let's start
by considering the connections that already exist between advocacy and teaching.
Teachers, we believe, are natural advocates. They advocate quietly all the time
for their students and for curricular choices. They come to understand the whole
students in front of them, recognize their strengths and challenges, and advocate
for their well-being and right to be educated. Teachers differentiate curricula for
students based on their students' individual needs, work with support teams within
their schools and communities, and explain to a host of others what students need
to be successful. As organizer Ernesto Cortés (1996) explains,

> Organizing is teaching. Like any organizer, a teacher stirs curiosity and imag-
> ination, connects to people and what's important to them, and teaches them
> how to acquire the capacity to pursue their inclinations and their imagination.
> Organizing is getting people to understand the meaning of things and how
> the world works—and then acting cooperatively on that understanding. (p. 7)

Another thing we know is that a number of teachers these days are taking on
the role of public advocate. We need look no further than the teachers in Chicago,
Oklahoma, West Virginia, and Los Angeles who organized, educated others, and
then went on strike over issues of school funding, student services, teacher pay,
class size, and more. And a few years earlier, teachers in Seattle struck over the
overreliance on and overabundance of standardized tests.

We also know many teachers who write public blogs, designed to help others understand the basis of literacy education. [Examples: *Citizen Teacher*, a blog written by high school teacher lisa eddy (https://citizenteacher.wordpress.com/about/); the *Teachers, Profs, Parents: Writers Who Care* blog written by teachers, parents, citizens, and professors (https://writerswhocare.wordpress.com/)] At a local level, we've worked with teachers who offer family literacy nights, parent book clubs, and content-based newsletters. Many teachers focus their advocacy efforts on their own students, introducing curricular practices that are place-based, problem-based, inquiry-based—designed to promote youth activism and create a new generation of students who name, study, and report on issues of interest in their own communities.

All these efforts are, quite frankly, amazing—given the climate of education in our country. Interestingly, however, not all of the teachers who do this work would call themselves advocates. Because, let's face it: even the word *advocacy* can seem a little scary, something that conjures up visions of Norma Rae jumping onto a work table and proudly holding up a sign emblazoned with the word "union" (before she gets carted off to jail), something that seems inspiring and kind of romantic—but also scarily job-threatening. Some teachers have tried to be advocates—marching, phoning legislators, writing letters and tweets—often becoming discouraged when the bill doesn't pass, their story isn't heard, the changes don't come. They begin to feel as if raising their voices did little good in impacting the status quo. Advocacy, they've learned from experience, can be frightening, disheartening, and discouraging.

What we want to suggest in this book is a slightly different way of thinking about advocacy, what we've come to call *everyday advocacy*. What's different about naming advocacy in this way? We see everyday advocacy as something teachers can do in their local settings to reset the story of education, the day-to-day actions teachers can take to change the public narrative regarding schools, teachers, and learning. At its core, everyday advocacy is teacher-centered and teacher-driven, designed by teachers to both lay the groundwork surrounding a particular issue and then respond appropriately when a contested issue turns into a problem. We think of everyday advocacy with a small "a," as opposed to capital "A" advocacy, which is often focused on producing sweeping legislative changes that are not designed by individual teachers, and that rely on large numbers to call for large-scale actions (see Figure 1.1).

While teachers can (and do) regularly join coalitions that focus on legislative advocacy, we see everyday advocacy as an important complement to that work and,

Figure 1.1 Everyday Advocacy versus Legislative Advocacy

Everyday Advocacy	Legislative Advocacy
The day-to-day actions teachers can take to change the public narrative surrounding schools, teachers, and learning	Actions usually undertaken by a larger group to make change: to support or oppose legislative action or candidates; to lobby for a cause
Proactive steps designed by teachers to lay the groundwork	Proactive steps usually designed by an organized group that invites others (like teachers) to participate
Action steps designed by teachers to create change on specific issues	Action steps usually focused on urging action in order to influence decision-makers

as you'll see in the pages of this book, a necessary component for change, one that is part of today's teacher professionalism.

As we suggest in Figure 1.1, everyday advocacy relies on both proactive and action-oriented steps. Proactive steps are those that can *casually educate* others before an issue even arises and those that can *intentionally educate* others on a specific teaching practice that might have the potential to be questioned by others. Action-oriented steps are those that *specifically focus* on a particular issue that is currently of concern.

Let's begin by considering what we mean by proactive steps, what we consider the first steps toward everyday advocacy. Proactive steps are what we can do as a matter of course to keep others informed—helping them become knowledgeable about current understandings of literacy as well as simply establishing meaningful connections with those who can impact how literacy is taught in a setting. These range from casual conversations to intentional outreach and are often directed at a variety of audiences, from colleagues and administrators to families and community members (see Figures 1.2 and 1.3).

Later in this chapter, we explain how these proactive steps intersect with action steps, but for now, just notice how these proactive measures can set the stage, introduce others to what the best research and practice tell us about literacy education, and do so in a low-stress manner. A number of teachers already practice many of these ideas, but they may not associate the practices with any kind of advocacy. We believe that helping teachers begin to see that establishing relationships

Figure 1.2 Proactive Steps: Casual

With Colleagues	With Administrators	With Families	With Community Members
Talking with colleagues at meetings, at lunch—going beyond talking with "the usual suspects"	Talking with administrators on a regular basis	Talking to parents at school events or before and after school	Inviting community members to classroom events that demonstrate current ways of thinking about literacy
Sharing an article you've recently read that introduces a new teaching approach	Sharing an article you've recently read that makes you think hard about how literacy is taught in your school	Creating newsletters about what students are doing that represents current understandings of literacy	Collaborating with local businesses to learn the kinds of reading and writing they commonly practice
Organizing a book club about current literacy research	Suggesting that administrators share an article regarding literacy with the department or faculty	Creating family message journals, in which students and parents write back and forth about their writing or reading	Inviting community members into the classroom to share their expertise and/or serve as an audience for student writing
Displaying in the hallways student projects that represent your vision of literacy	Inviting administrators into your classroom to see effective literacy practices in action	Organizing family literacy nights focused on reading, writing, and other literacy practices	Use social media to educate others about issues surrounding literacy and literacy pedagogy

with others and introducing others to some basic understanding of literacy and research-based best practices in ways that are neither preachy nor heavy-handed are indeed the first steps toward changing the narrative about teachers, teaching, and learning—and as such, these acts are a form of advocacy. And as you'll see in the sections that follow, teachers who practice these measures as a matter of

Figure 1.3 Proactive Steps: Intentional

With Families	With Administrators	With the Larger World
A narrative about the value of a particular curricular approach →	*A narrative about the value of a particular curricular approach* →	*A narrative about the value of a particular curricular approach* →
Create videos of your classroom, demonstrating how students learn and how you teach, for parents	Share a video or an article that focuses on a curricular practice you'd like to implement in your school	Start your own blog about the curricular approach, share others' blog posts on the topic, and respond to others' blogs
A narrative about choice reading and the value of Young Adult (YA) literature →	*A narrative about choice reading and YA literature* →	*A narrative about choice reading and YA literature* →
Set up YA book clubs with parents	Share videos and research findings about choice literature and its impact on student reading	Create your own videos or share videos of students at work (only with written permissions)
A narrative about student writing →	*A narrative about student writing* →	*A narrative about student writing* →
Invite parents to student-led portfolio nights	Share videos and research findings about inquiry-based writing and its impact on student writing	Be active on social media, re-posting news about student writing with references to your story

course in their teaching are more successful when they begin to target an issue that they deem important.

Throughout this work, we have come to rely on three core ideas surrounding advocacy that have informed both how we talk about advocacy and how we work with teachers:

1. The importance of story
2. The importance of identifying and framing an issue
3. The importance of grassroots, situational approaches to change

Core Idea 1: The Importance of Story

Many people in the world tell stories about teachers and schools—on the sidelines of soccer games, in the grocery line, in state legislatures, in blogs and tweets and newspaper stories, in movies and television shows. Stories like these contribute to a public narrative that gradually takes on a kind of truth in the world, a truth that is mostly narrated by outsiders to the world of classrooms and teachers and students. This narrative is used to mandate curriculum, create policy, and even pass laws that in turn create further "truths," such as:

- *Teachers don't know how to teach; therefore, curricula must be developed by companies who are "experts" in education; thus, teachers must follow pacing guides and mandated daily lesson plans.*
- *Students in urban areas don't know how to learn; standardized tests show this; thus, in order to improve/eliminate these schools, we must "grade" schools based on these tests. That way, the public knows which are good schools and which are bad schools.*
- *Most teachers don't care about their students; they just teach because the hours are good and they have summers off, except for that one superstar teacher who defies all odds (and, we would add, systemic structural inequities) by working 80 hours a week to save students; thus, the only "good" teachers are those who work in this way.*
- *Education schools only think about theory and aren't preparing teachers to be successful; thus, we should shut them down and rethink how to educate teachers. Alternative certification programs are the answer.*
- *(And, what may be the most damning of them all) Everyone knows what's involved in teaching because we all went to school ourselves; anyone can teach because it's not that hard; therefore, it's not a "real" profession like medicine or law.*

The images that arise from these stories are pervasive, and the results are devastating to teachers, to kids and to the educational system. As we noted at the beginning of this chapter, fewer and fewer college students are going into teaching, and too many of those who stay in the field of teaching stay for too short a period of time. (Which, as a side note, creates another story about teachers: the diminishing number of teachers who stay in education is seen as evidence of the problematic nature of colleges of education—except when referring to teachers from programs like "Teach for America," who are *expected* to stay only two years but are lauded for their brief service in helping to "save" kids.)

What would happen, however, if another story of education contributed to the public narrative—the actual story of teachers told by teachers themselves? This idea of shifting the public narrative is the basis of work developed by Marshall Ganz, a long-time community organizer and senior lecturer at Harvard. Ganz begins with this idea: storytelling is at the center of change. Ganz (2011, p. 282) explains, "Storytelling is how we interact with each other about values; how we share experiences with each other, counsel each other, comfort each other, and inspire each other to action." There is a great power in storytelling, Ganz believes, because

> It's a fundamental way in which we understand who we are in the world . . . . [T]he construction of narrative is a piece of identity work that provides us with moral resources to make choices in a world full of uncertainty. (Global Academy Media, 2019)

According to Ganz, creating that narrative requires connecting the head and the heart:

> [T]he challenge here is how to access those emotional resources that enable mindful action, that enable action with intentionality. Now stories are the way in which we learn to do that because a story is really a moment of agency. In other words, what makes a story a story, a plot, is a protagonist is confronted with a challenge for which he or she is unprepared and then has to deal with. And then they struggle to deal with it and then it produces an outcome and then there is a moral that we get from that. Now because we can identify empathetically with the protagonist, we can experience the content of the story . . . . And so by identifying with the protagonist, the moral we draw is a moral to the heart, not just to the head. (Global Academy Media, 2019)

We've found that Ganz's emphasis on story is particularly appealing to teachers of literacy. Ganz focuses on the idea of a *public narrative* as the means by which an issue comes to be understood in a community, a narrative that draws upon the story elements we know so well: plot, characters, setting, and morals.

This notion of a public narrative is complex, though. It is much more than the telling of an individual story, a trope teachers (and others) too often rely on to help the public understand the story of education (i.e., the story of Teacher X, who overcame great obstacles to reach these difficult children, or the story of Teacher Y, whose classroom practices show us the "true" story of urban education). Ganz's idea of the public narrative moves beyond the individual, sometimes idiosyncratic story, emphasizing three parts: the story of self, the story of us, and the story of now.

- **Story of Self:** Ganz sees our individual stories as where we begin—not where we end. *The story of self*—our own story of teaching and learning—helps us begin to identify the values that inform our understanding. And for Ganz, understanding the values that underlie our story is what's truly important.

- **Story of Us:** Ganz's next step is for us to talk to other like-minded people about all of our stories of self. As we talk and share our individual stories, he suggests, we can then identify the values we hold in common, the ideas that cross these idiosyncratic stories. *The story of us* becomes more powerful than an individual story because it places our unique anecdotes in a larger context, helping us claim, for example, that the stories of teachers everywhere have commonality, have inherent values, have meaning and purpose.

- **Story of Now:** This is the action step, where our shared stories and values lead us to move forward and make change. *The story of now* asks us to think about what we do with this collective knowledge and how this knowledge can help us change the current narrative into one that is truly public. *The story of now* relies on the expertise that exists in both individual and collective stories and puts the onus for change not on a heroic individual but on the collective efforts of an entire community.

In some of his writings and workshops, Ganz illustrates the public narrative through then Senator Barack Obama's famous keynote speech at the 2004 Democratic Convention. (You might want to view the first eight minutes of this speech as you read the next part.) Obama begins the speech by telling his *story of self*, sharing his parents' and grandparents' background, identifying their dreams and their "abiding faith in the possibilities of this nation." He moves to the *story of us* as he calls upon the values inherent in those dreams and the diversity of his heritage to proclaim, "My story is part of the larger American story . . . In no other country on Earth is my story even possible." Through brief vignettes that reference the stories of other Americans, he speaks to these shared values, values he links to the Declaration of Independence as the foundational document of our nation: that is, we can say what we think, start our own business, participate in the political process without fear of retribution. Building on the *story of self and the story of us*, he then turns to *the story of now*, a callout to Democrats, Republicans, and Independents, saying that if we share those values, we have more work to do together (in the case of this speech, to work hard to elect Kerry).

In our workshops with teachers, we often draw upon the first eight minutes of this speech to demonstrate how the three kinds of stories work together. We invite teachers to watch the speech, analyzing how the stories of self, us, and now function in it and how the natural progression of these three stories seeks to create a new public narrative. We then invite teachers to try this themselves, based in their own stories of teaching. We offer the prompts in Figure 1.4 to help them through the process. Figure 1.5 shows the thinking of one teacher group who tried this.

Stories, we contend, are an important starting point for this advocacy work. In a low-stakes way, teachers begin to identify themselves as knowledgeable narrators of their own experience in schools and to understand the shared values that will resonate with others.[*]

---

[*] One teacher who has gone through our workshop recently added the important work of Chimamanda Ngozi Adichie to our discussion of story. Adichie's 2009 TedTalk "The Danger of a Single Story" has quickly become a classic for teachers and speaks to both the importance of storytelling and the problems that arise when one story becomes *the* story (https://www.ted .com/talks/chimamanda_adichie_the_danger_of_a_single_story).

Core Idea 2: The Importance of Identifying and Framing an Issue

It's understandable that when teachers get together to talk about "the problems in education" (and we include ourselves in this characterization), we do at least two things: First, we tend to focus on the big issues, the issues that seem to overwhelm us, the issues that seem too pervasive for us to have any influence over, often the things that we can't seem to figure out how to change: standardized testing, mandated curriculum, censorship . . . the list goes on and on. And second, we talk about these issues in a kind of shorthand—through the lens of the shared values mentioned in the previous section. In other words, as teach-

Figure 1.4 Story of Self, Us, and Now

Story of self. Write for a few minutes about an individual story of teaching, one that reflects a successful teaching moment. After you write, look back at the story and think about two sets of questions:

- What made it successful? Were there challenges involved in reaching that success? What are the *values* that underlie the success of that moment?
- How does that moment compare to the current narrative on public education? Does it rely on the same values that underlie the narrative? If not, what's different?

Story of us. In small groups, share your stories, and think together about these questions:

- What *themes* do you notice across these stories?
- What *values* do you share?
- What *key terms* arise?
- How does hearing someone else's story help you make sense of larger issues?

Story of now. Think together about where these stories lead us and how they might help someone understand a different story of teaching. This is where we start to get into the nitty-gritty of organizing.

- With whom could/should we share our story?
- What about our story would resonate with our audience?
- What specifics would be convincing?
- What genres for sharing would best speak to our audience?

Figure 1.5 One Teacher Group's Story of Us

ers and teacher educators, we share insider knowledge and insider language, so that when we mention student choice or formative assessment or project-based learning, we have in common a general understanding of what we mean by those terms. It's important to remember, however, that the general public—those we want to reach out to—probably don't share that same knowledge. Thus, when we speak in one way, those who are outside of our shared-values group (perhaps parents, administrators, community members, legislators—maybe even other teachers in our setting) might hear our words in a different way from what we intend.

The second core idea—identifying and framing an issue—helps us overcome that communication gap. It becomes, in essence, a means of narrowing and focusing advocacy efforts to find ways to communicate that focus to others. Based in both communication theory and organizing theory, the idea behind identifying and framing is this: People are not blank slates; in fact, everyone already has particular frames through which they understand issues, frames that connect to their deeply held values and worldviews. (Think back to the story of self. For most of us, our own story is set in a particular way of thinking; that way informs so much about how we understand the world.) It's important for us to understand the frames that people bring to an issue because all communication that people receive is perceived through their own frames. In other words, while I might be talking about point *x* through my particular frame (a frame that goes back to the values I hold), someone else will hear the point I'm making through their already existing frame and the values they hold and thus understand it differently from how I intend it to be understood. Specifically, when we talk about schools, most people bring a frame to their understanding of education: a frame that has been formed over the years through their own experiences as students themselves; in many cases, through the experiences of their own children; and through what they hear and see in books, movies, television, and social media.

Given this, how do we change the current frames that surround a particular way of thinking? First, we have to identify the frames that exist around a particular issue and understand why these frames have been effective at informing people's mindsets. (Back to the example of schools: if someone's frame around the teaching of writing harkens back to their own education, when they wrote single-draft, five-paragraph essays that were read by their teachers, marked in red pen, and assigned a grade, they most likely will not understand what those of us with a workshop, multimodal process frame mean when we use the term *writing*.) Then, we must find ways to create new frames that might help others understand an issue differently. (Again, to extend the example above: a new frame might call upon people's more recent experiences in writing in workplace, civic, and personal settings, focusing on the multiple approaches writers take, depending on the audience and the purpose of the writing.) At the center of framing and reframing is recognition of *who* you want to reach, *what* their prior experience has been, and *how* you might hone in on the issue in a way that will make sense to that audience.

Popular Frame of Education	Reframe
Teacher as hero, who single-handedly saves students	Teacher as part of a larger system that relies on the intersection of parts to provide a strong education for students
College readiness as a series of discrete and linear skills	College readiness as habits of mind
Students as recipients of knowledge imparted by teachers	Students as active participants in creating knowledge

Reframing is the key to shifting the narrative surrounding education—because so often the current frame just seems like common sense to many people. Think for a moment about these examples of frames and reframes:

Or consider this wonderful example of framing and reframing that we read in Peter Greene's (2019) *Curmudgucation* blog "Why It's Important to Say There Is No Teacher Shortage." He posits, if we accept the frame, *we've got a teacher shortage*, we are assuming that " 'teacher' is some sort of solid genetic state that either exists or does not, and if there aren't enough of them, well, shrug, whatcha gonna do?" The resultant action is to search for a Band-Aid for the problem, grasping for some kind of teacher substitutes—in particular, to lower the bar for who is qualified to teach. But if we shift the frame to "Teaching has become such unattractive work that few people want to do it," we also shift the focus to look more closely at the systemic issues surrounding education that contribute to this frame: treating teachers with respect, giving them autonomy and authority. Changing the frame, in other words, changes the narrative of the problem and, consequently, of the solution.

One resource we have come to rely on to help teachers understand the idea of framing is the FrameWorks Institute, an online resource that provides training and support on how to do this work. In particular, their free training *Changing the Public Conversation on Social Problems: A Beginner's Guide to Strategic Frame Analysis* (FrameWorks Institute, 2009) takes you through a process of learning about communications theory and its connection to social change, ways to tell a public story through an impactful frame, and how to evaluate the impact of your work. They also provide information on framing issues in new ways to speak to a greater audience.

What we've learned from the FrameWorks training and other communications and organizing theory is that when we identify and frame our issue, we (1) narrow our focus from a *general concern* (e.g., testing is bad) to a *specific issue* (e.g., teaching to the test leads to overemphasis on a very narrow set of skills) and (2) figure out what public misunderstanding allows this concern to persist. We then are able to reframe the issue and, in language that might appeal to others, help them rethink their frames.

We recognize that because the current narrative is filled with so many misconceptions about teachers and schools and public education, it's easy for us to feel overwhelmed. Because we feel passionate about all kinds of concerns that are impacting our lives and the lives of our students, we sometimes want to address all of the concerns, all at once. However, if we really want to make an effective contribution to changing a narrative, we need to focus on some part of the whole that we want the public to understand better. We suggest that teachers select an issue while keeping the following two thoughts in mind: (1) choose something that impacts you in your particular circumstances and local contexts, and (2) choose something that is within your power to change. Articulating a concern, narrowing it to something manageable, and then framing it in a way that will speak to others is the beginning of creating Ganz's *story of now*, a first step toward making strategic change. (And just to foreshadow a bit: later in this chapter, you will be able to read how some teachers have selected and framed an issue, pushing forward to create change.)

It is important to remember that narrowing one's large concerns to a single issue doesn't mean that we have to reduce the complexity of a particular topic, nor do we have to ignore the inter-relatedness of many educational concerns. Rather, it means focusing on one thing at a time, realizing that we can turn to another issue in the future.

When we work with teachers, we begin by asking them to complete the online training from FrameWorks Institute—and to occasionally pause the training to talk about the ideas it offers and how those ideas connect to their own work. We then ask them to work toward identifying and naming their issue by following a series of steps (see Figure 1.6).

As teachers move through these steps, they find ways to connect their personal stories and shared values to an issue they care deeply about. By focusing on the

Figure 1.6 Identifying and Framing an Issue: Steps for Teachers

Step 1: Identify a concern. What is the burning issue about teaching, learning, students, or literacy that keeps you up at night? What is the part of it that impacts you the most? Try to move from the broad topic to a more narrow and focused issue.

Step 2: Narrow the concern. Focus on an issue that connects to your context and to the values you talked about in the public narrative exercise. In other words, think about how your issue connects to student voice and choice or creating safe spaces or community building.

Step 3: Frame the issue. Think about how the issue is framed at present (think about news articles you've read, movies you've watched, what you've heard others say about it on the sidelines of soccer games or at a dinner party). What do you understand about the issue, and how do you see others understanding it? Ask yourself: What do I want the public to understand in order to create a change? How does my understanding of the issue connect to the public's? How can I present my concern in a way that will speak to the public's understanding?

Example:

Step 1: Identify a concern. Standardized testing

Step 2: Narrow the concern. What are your context and values? How does standardized testing most influence your school? How does it misalign with the collective values shared by teachers of literacy?

Step 3: Frame and cut the issue to reach your audience. Try out slightly different frames (often referred to as *cuts* in the organizing world) to see how you could speak to the audience you most want to reach:

> *Cut 1*: To community: Standardized testing promotes certain ways of thinking and kids who grow up in a context of multiple-choice responses will not truly become the active, flexible, critically thinking citizens or workers we need.
> *Cut 2*: To parents: Standardized testing takes away too many weeks of school each year, time that could be better spent with actual instruction.
> *Cut 3*: To administrators: Assessing teachers on a student's performance on a single standardized test is an unfair picture of a teacher's quality.

specific audiences and the frames that might appeal to each audience, the teachers begin to recognize how they can reach out to others to change the conversation about education. This background work sets the stage for the next core idea, in which teachers consider how to create an action plan surrounding their issue.

Core Idea 3: The Importance of Grassroots and Situational Approaches to Change

How do we move from sharing our stories and values (Core Idea 1) to identifying and framing our issues (Core Idea 2) to actually creating change? This third core idea immerses us in the worlds of community and grassroots organizing, especially as adapted from the work of respected groups and movements, such as the Midwest Academy, Beautiful Trouble, Harvard's Resistance School, and others. At its center, taking action simply means moving from that casual conversation (or rant!) with a colleague or trusted friend ("I wish I could change how *x* is done in my school.") to a specific path to create change—most often set in a local context surrounding a local issue.

We know that the idea of taking action to create change is a complicated one for teachers. We understand the hesitations, from "I'm not good at talking to adults about these issues" to "I'm not an expert" to "I don't have time to take on one more thing." And we also understand that, at times, what is considered "taking action" has led teachers to feel discouraged about this kind of work. This is especially likely to happen when we move immediately to tactics without thinking about an overall plan and the place of those tactics within that plan. In other words, we often—with the best of intentions—eagerly write letters to legislators, publish a blog, or testify at a school board meeting without always considering how these tactics could be part of a larger plan. And while there is certainly nothing wrong with these tactics— in fact these tactics can be very useful parts of an action plan—when they are done in an isolated way, they may not be as useful as we hope. Sometimes teachers (and, really, all activists) may feel dismay after employing isolated tactics: "Well, I wrote to my congressman, and nothing happened," or "I testified in front of the State Board of Education, and no one listened."Our message is not to meant to discourage teacher action, but rather to encourage teachers to think more about the *how* of action—how teachers can make these actions as impactful as they need to be.

When we look at the many occasions in which teacher actions have made a marked difference—occasions that we've read about in news stories and heard about in the stories of individual teachers who have gone through our workshops—we notice a common thread: These effective teachers employed what organizers refer to as an *action plan*—a structured, often step-by-step, approach to creating change, one that builds awareness, finds allies, stays on point, discovers who is in charge, celebrates short-term achievement, and identifies appropriate tactics. A wonderful case-in-point is the organizing work of the Parkland students following the horrific shooting in their high school. According to David Hines (2018), writing in *The Federalist*, the students' response to their situation "was professionalized. That's not surprising, because *this is what organization that gets results actually looks like. It's not a bunch of magical kids in somebody's living room*" [italics added]. Lisa Miller (2018), in a piece in *New York Magazine* called "The War Room," offered a compelling portrait of the careful and strategic approach these students took to organizing, as they moved from their own experiences as victims of a school shooting to reaching outward to educate and inform others of what changes could be made to prevent this in the future. In the article, Miller describes the time she spent with the students in the aftermath of the shooting, highlighting what the students learned about advocacy and how they worked together to create a message and employed multiple tactics to get the message across.

In our work with teachers, we break down some of what successful organizers and advocates suggest, naming a number of *action principles*, designed to help teachers see this work as incremental but with a long-term goal in mind. The action principles we identify are not set rules or steps to be taken in a particular order,

Figure 1.7 Action Principles

- Build awareness
- Find allies
- Stay on point

- Think long-term; Celebrate short-term
- Discover who's in charge
- Identify tactics

but rather the principles are designed to give teachers some ways of thinking about change-making that grow from their authentic concerns and their own settings. What follows are the descriptions of these action principles.

Action Principle 1: Build Awareness

Advocacy can begin long before we have a specific action plan in mind. It begins when we want to educate others more generally about issues surrounding education or—in Ganz's terms—when we want to change the public narrative. One way to create a different narrative is to be proactive about what we do as teachers, why we do it, and how we do it.

When we are proactive, we are "sowing the seeds of change." We reach out to others around us—colleagues, administrators, parents, others in the community—to share with them a vision of what literacy education can look like. We invite them into conversations with us, gently sharing something exciting that a student has achieved, showing them a vision of a classroom practice, asking them what they notice: in other words, providing them with what might be an alternate view.

This kind of proactive work is designed to help others understand the values that underlie what we're doing, to see what kids can achieve when these ways of literacy education become the classroom norm, and to imagine a different way of thinking about school and literacy.

Action Principle 2: Find Allies

One of the first lessons of advocacy work is that it's easier and more effective if we do this work with others. When we share our individual stories with others, we are sharing the underlying values that might help them join us to make sustained change; the more people who join together in a cause, the greater the chance of changing others' minds.

The key to this collaborative work is *finding allies*. Allies are those people who share our beliefs and values about an issue—but allies are not always those who are the most vocal or the most obvious. Often times we discover potential allies who are invested in similar issues. Allies might grow out of the work you've done in sowing the seeds of change: a colleague who noticed your classroom library and asks some questions about why you have so many books, a parent who attended a literacy night and sends you an email wanting to know more, an administrator who heard from a parent about your teaching.

As everyday advocate and school librarian Beth Shaum explains,

In my twelve years of teaching, it took me a while to realize this, but parents are your biggest allies. Sometimes we focus so much on what is happening in our classrooms that we can erroneously view parents as our adversaries. But think about how quickly news travels when parents aren't happy with something that is happening in your school. Use that power to your advantage. Ask yourself: Who are the powerful voices? Who are the changemakers? Go so far as to be part of your school's parent-teacher organization, so when you do find yourself needing something, you don't have to start from scratch; you've already built important relationships to help make change happen. Having parents on your side can also provide an important buffer if your school has a particularly toxic administration and you need people to go to bat for you. When you partner with parents, change often happens more quickly than if you ally only with other teachers.

Action Principle 3: Stay on Point

In the current educational landscape, it's easy to get overwhelmed! Because we see so much need for change in so many areas, we can find ourselves distracted by the most current and immediate problem, so much so that it's hard to stay on point. So, what can we do to keep ourselves focused and on point?

Step 1: Find your issue. One way to find your issue is to think about these questions:

- What do you most wish others understood about literacy? About literacy pedagogy? Why do you think they don't understand it?
- What gets in the way of teaching literacy in the ways you want to teach it? What supports successful ways of teaching literacy?
- What have your students shown you about literacy and literacy learning that you wish others understood?
- If you could recreate how literacy is taught in your school, what would you focus on?
- Who are you as a teacher? What are your values? How did you come to believe in those values?

Step 2: Narrow your issue. The next step is to narrow your issue. We've found two approaches particularly helpful for teachers in the narrowing process: reduce the issue to a 90-second elevator speech (which we write, rehearse, and then practice on each other) or reduce the issue to visual representations (like bumper stickers or memes) that cut to the essence of the issue. Both of these might later serve as tactics, but at this point the purpose is to use creative means to narrow and focus.

Action Principle 4: Think Long-Term; Celebrate Short-Term

While many of us would like to wave our magic wands and transform literacy education *right away*, one of the most important lessons of advocacy work is that change takes time. Those big goals we've set for ourselves—the goals that seem to define true change—are important to keep in mind as what we imagine we'd like to achieve in the long term. But basing our success at advocacy solely on these long-term goals can lead us to feel discouraged and frustrated. In part, it's because these goals are often a little too lofty ("getting rid of standardized testing" or "having teachers treated with more respect"), noble aims, for sure, but not really within our power as a teacher or group of teachers. We suggest that teachers think about the long-term, but also consider the interim steps to get there.

Step 1: Articulate a clear and achievable long-term goal by focusing on what you *want* to accomplish, what you *can* accomplish, and what change would *actually look like.* We urge teachers to be honest about what they think they can achieve in their particular context, especially given that full-time job they have as teachers.

Step 2: Work backward from that goal, focusing on the short-term and intermediate goals that would help gather momentum to reach the long-term goal, building awareness among others about the goal, and considering who might be allies to join in the work.

Step 3: Define what success means, especially in terms of short-term goals. As we've learned from a number of long-time organizers, we do have choices when we do this work, and we have the power to determine what constitutes success. Each time we succeed in a goal, we gain confidence to move on to the next one.

Thinking of advocacy work as a journey, as a means toward an end and not as an end in itself, can lead teachers to celebrate the short-term goals and see them as concrete ways to reach the larger goals.

Action Principle 5: Discover Who's in Charge

To make change real and lasting, teachers need to learn about the decision-making process in their school or district: *how* decisions are made, *who* makes the decisions, and *who might have influence* on those decision-makers. The last point is where the proactive work of building awareness and finding allies pays off. If we have been successful in creating a culture of shared values and we've developed strong allies, we have many people (parents, other teachers, community members) who either may have influence with decision-makers or who know of others they can call upon to wield their influence. Remember, sometimes we have to step back and realize that the message is better received by a decision-maker when it comes through the voice of an ally rather than a teacher.

As an example, if your issue is *building a culture of choice in how reading is taught*, you may discover that a particular committee in your school is charged with choosing new mandatory professional development (PD) opportunities surrounding reading instruction. Because you know that the PD that is selected will inform how school-wide mandated curriculum develops around reading instruction, you identify that committee as one of your decision-makers.

The most direct way to influence these decision-makers would be to join that committee and become part of the team of decision-makers. However, if that is not a possibility, you may still be influential in other ways: you may be able to encourage one of your allies to join the committee or you might develop allies among those already on the committee, sharing with them alternative ways of thinking about reading instruction and suggesting books, authors, video, or online PD that might show them the research behind the way you are thinking.

Action Principle 6: Identify Tactics

Tactics are those specific actions that we take to try to create change. And there are many kinds of tactics, from sending a tweet to a congressional representative to inviting parents to watch a video of our classroom. What does this mean for your own work? If you're focusing on a particular issue and message that you've developed, your tactics might take one of two forms (that we alluded to earlier in the chapter), both serving an important purpose in moving forward: tactics designed to lay the groundwork (what we sometimes call *proactive tactics*) and tactics designed to influence a particular decision point (what we sometimes refer to as *calls to action*).

Tactics to lay the groundwork. Tactics that lay the groundwork help others understand general concepts or specific stances: they can be those things we do on a day-to-day basis to help others better understand our classroom practice, our reasons for teaching in the ways we do, or our stances on specific educational ideas—in other words, those approaches to building awareness.

For example, when we write a letter to parents explaining our curriculum, we're using a tactic that lays the groundwork—helping to inform them about our ways of teaching. When we host a literacy night in which we invite parents to think about the reading and writing they do in their everyday lives and then connect that to what we're teaching, we're using a tactic that lays the groundwork. Much of what teachers can do to try to change the public narrative about education might begin with tactics like these.

Tactics to influence a particular decision point. Tactics that are designed to influence others at a particular decision point essentially demand action. When we testify at a school board meeting about cutting budgets for a library or getting rid of creative writing classes, or when we meet with the curriculum committee to suggest an alternative use for textbook money—to purchase young adult fiction—we are practicing calls to action. These tactics target a particular issue, inform the decision maker about the issue, and then suggest something the decision maker might do to create change. In part, these tactics are informative, but the underlying goal is to motivate the decision-makers to do something with the information you've provided. These tactics are usually well-thought out and directly connect to some of the action principles raised thus far: finding allies and discovering who's in charge; framing and cutting the issue; and considering short-term, intermediate, and long-term goals.

Putting It All together: Creating Action Plans

As the educators we work with immerse themselves in these three core ideas (the importance of story, the importance of identifying and framing an issue, and the importance of grassroots and situational approaches to change), they begin the process of determining the specifics for what they might do to move forward. We build upon these principles to create an action plan, a concrete rendering of their next steps. Action plans, in other words, move us from idea to action. Building upon the six Action Principles above, action plans include:

- Proactive advocacy principles designed to help create an atmosphere conducive to change (*building awareness* and *finding allies*)
- Principles for moving from a broad concern to a more defined issue (*staying on point* and *identifying long term and short-term goals*)
- Principles for targeting your approach (*discovering who's in charge* and *identifying tactics*)
- Action plans, in other words, help us all to move beyond a "just-tactics" mentality and to see advocacy as more than a one-shot movement.

Strategy and Tactics

Action plans, we explain to teachers, consist of two connected parts: the overall strategy underlying the work and the tactics needed to put that work into practice. What's the difference between these two components? A strategy statement is a basic building block of advocacy. It defines who you want to reach, what you want them to understand differently, and what you ultimately hope to achieve through your advocacy. Strategy statements are realistic and focused explanations of our work that help ground us as advocates, and we can return to them time and again.

Strategy: To get them started creating these statements, we usually invite teachers to immerse themselves in some strategy statements written by others and we offer them a template: *How to effectively tell [X message] to [Y audience] to achieve [Z result].* We define those three variables in this way:

- **Message**: What it is you want others to know, how you can cut it to reach the people you need to reach, and the context
- **Audience**: Who you want to reach (decision-makers; allies; opponents and undecideds) and how you'll shape the message for each of them
- **Results**: The goals you hope to achieve in the short-, intermediate-, and long-term—the timeline for your plan

When we work with teachers, we reserve as much time as it takes to complete the writing of these statements because we realize that the process requires careful thought, feedback, and revision in order to write something concise, focused, and effective. We also share strategy statements created by other teachers for their own advocacy work, such as:

> In order to create lifelong, engaged readers who have the literacy skills they need for college and workplace success, teachers, administrators, and parents need to work together to promote a vibrant and well-supported reading community in our school. (Alaina Feliks, high school teacher)

> If we want to empower students to read and to create a buzz about reading in our school, we need to show the administration we need a more vibrant school library. (Kris Gedeon, high school teacher)

Strategy statements can help us identify appropriate tactics: the specific actions you take to successfully advocate for the changes you seek. Organizers generally have multiple tactics that may be designed to reach different audiences. What's most important in devising tactics, we tell teachers, is that you choose those that you feel comfortable enacting and that you can imagine doing as part of a journey toward change.

Tactics: We also devote a lot of time to tactics in our workshops, talking about proactive and responsive tactics and the reasons why certain tactics work better than others in particular situations. We connect these tactics to strategy statements, emphasizing that while a certain tactic might be comfortable for them, it may not be the best one to further their strategy statement—and thus their campaign. Tactics, in other words, must fit into a strategy statement, offering the best ways to effectively get a message out to a particular audience. Most campaigns involve multiple tactics, directed toward different audiences, which is another point we emphasize with teachers.

The next step in the process is for teachers to create an action plan. Action plans are important summaries of their best thinking to this point, they are aspirational plans for what comes next and recursive spaces for reconsideration and redirection. Action plans are not designed to be set in stone but rather to be flexible as conditions change. Yet, as constant reminders of what can be achieved, they have the potential to keep us focused.

Templates 1 and 2 at the end of the chapter demonstrate what we mean by actions plans: Template 1 is an example for creating an action plan, and Template 2 is a completed action plan, based on that example, written by high school teacher Alaina Feliks. You can also follow up on Alaina's work in Part II of this book where she describes what happened as she put her plan into effect.

Why This Immersion Into Everyday Advocacy?

In this chapter, our goal has been to introduce you to the reasons we believe advocacy must be a vital part of teacher education—both for preservice teachers and those who have been practicing for years. And we have done a deep dive into everyday advocacy, sharing the approaches we have taken in workshops and professional learning experiences and sharing the ways teachers have embraced these approaches. Before you read the next chapters, we ask that you step back and take a moment to consider how our discussion relates to your own work as an English educator or teacher leader. You might think about questions like these:

- What conditions are part of your teachers' and preservice teachers' lives?
- What is the narrative regarding education in general and regarding literacy education in their contexts?
- Are teachers' voices a part of that narrative?
- What literacy education issues do you think others (administrators, families, community members) would benefit from learning more about?
- Who might help others learn about those issues?
- Who are the decision-makers on these issues in your area?
- What role could you take—as a literacy educator, professional learning leader, National Writing Project teacher consultant, or teacher leader—to promote advocacy?

These questions help set the stage for what comes next in the book. In the chapters that follow, we will immerse you even more in the worlds of advocacy as we share the voices of teachers and teacher educators who are doing this work in many different ways. As you answer these questions and read what these teachers are doing, we ask you to remember this: There is no one way to do advocacy. The work of advocacy is never formulaic or exacting. It should constantly be made and remade depending on the context of particular communities, the comfort level of teachers (although we have seen teachers find their comfort level increases the more they do this work), and the politics surrounding the specific issues of concern. Getting into the mindset of advocacy, acknowledging that advocacy could become a part of our day-to-day lives as well as the lives of the teachers with whom we work, is a huge step—and a great place to begin. Remember the words of middle school teacher Jeff Taylor that opened this chapter, "As educators, our collective voices hold awesome power. When we follow the methods of everyday advocacy, we portray a succinct message that not only has staying power but opens the doors for action."

References

Adichie, C. N. (2009). *Chimamanda Ngozi Adichie: The danger of a single story* [Video file]. Retrieved from https://www.ted.com/talks/chimamanda_adichie_the_danger _of_a_single_story

Cortés, E. (1996). Interview with Dave Winans. *NEA Today* (May):7

Council for the Accreditation of Educator Preparation. (n.d.). Standard 1: Content and pedagogical knowledge. Retrieved from http://caepnet.org/standards/standard-1

FrameWorks Institute. (2009). http://sfa.frameworksinstitute.org/

Ganz, M. (2011). Public narrative, collective action, and power. In Odugbemi, S. & Lee, T. (Eds.), Accountability through public opinion: From inertia to public action (pp. 273–289). Washington DC: The World.

Global Academy Media (2019). Transcript—Marshall Ganz: *The power of storytelling* in dialogue with Walter Link. Retrieved from http://www.globalacademy.media/ transcript-marshall-ganz-the-power-of-storytelling/

Green, P. (2019). Why it's important to say there is no teacher shortage. *Curmudgucation: Trying to make sense of what's happening in education.* Retrieved from http:// curmudgucation.blogspot.com/2019/04/why-its-important-to-say-there-is-no.html

Hines, D. (2018). Why did it take two weeks to discover Parkland students' astroturfing? *The Federalist.* Retrieved from http://thefederalist.com/2018/03/01/take-two-weeks -truth-emerge-parkland-students-astroturfing/

Ingersoll, R. M., Merrill, E., Stuckey, D., & Collins, G. (2018). Seven trends: The transformation of the teaching force – Updated October 2018. *CPRE Research Reports.* Retrieved from https://repository.upenn.edu/cpre_researchreports/108

King, J. (2018). *Colleges of education: A national portrait.* AACTE.

Miller, L. (2018). The war room, *New York Magazine.* Retrieved from (http://nymag.com/ intelligencer/2018/03/on-the-ground-with-parkland-teens-as-they-plot-a-revolution .html?gtm=bottom&gtm=bottom)

Rich, M. (2016). Why Teachers on TV Have to Be Incompetent or Inspiring. *New York Times*. Retrieved from https://www.nytimes.com/2016/04/10/opinion/sunday/why-teachers-on-tv-have-to-be-incompetent-or-inspiring.html

Thomas, A. (n.d.).Why Teachers Quit. *The Quad*. Retrieved from https://thebestschools.org/magazine/why-teachers-quit/

Template 1: Everyday Advocacy: Creating an Action Plan

Use this planning sheet to help you think through your issue and create an action plan.

Step 1: Background
The Concern:
- What is the big picture problem?

The Issue:
- How does that big picture problem relate to your own situation?
- What is your specific situation?
- How is the issue situated in your own context?
- What about the issue is within your power to change?

The Frames:
- How is this issue currently framed in the public's consciousness?
- What kind of frame would better communicate your issue?

Step 2: Strategy
Who is your audience?
- Who are the decision-makers for your issue?
- Are those decision-makers the main audience?
- Is there a secondary audience that would be important to reach?
- Who are your allies? Opponents? Undecideds?
- How will you shape your message to reach each group?

What is your message?
- How can you translate your issue into a statement that will move your audience to action?
- How can you cut or frame your statement to reach the people you need to reach?
- What is the context for your message?

What results do you hope for?
- What change are you seeking?
- What is your long-term goal?
- What are some immediate and short-term goals that will help you reach the long-term goal?
- How will you know you were successful?
- What is your timeline?

Write your strategy in a one-sentence statement:
- How to effectively tell *X message* to *Y audience* to achieve *Z result*.

Step 3: Tactics
- What actions will you take to create change surrounding your issue?
- Which tactics make the most sense in the short-term, intermediate, and long-term?
- Which tactics fit for particular audiences? Are you seeking to inform, change minds, inspire action, or something else?

This chart might work as a template for your planning:

Goals	Audience(s) for That Goal	Allies? Opponents? Undecideds?	Cut/ Frame for That Audience	Tactics	Time Frame
Short-term					
Intermediate					
Long-term					

Template 2: Alaina Feliks' Action Plan

Strategy Statement: In order to create lifelong, engaged readers who have the literacy skills they need for college and workplace success, teachers, administrators, and parents need to work together to promote a vibrant and well-supported reading community in our school.

Short-Term Tactics:

Audience: Parents

1. Create an infographic to hand out at open house with a few facts about the importance of reading and things that parents can do to help.
   - Donate used books/magazines to the media center
   - Purchase books for the library from the public Amazon wish list
   - Donate money to the GoFundMe for the media center
   - Volunteer to do a book talk for the video library or share your reading on social media at #StockbridgeReads
   - Make reading a priority for your student! Help them set aside quiet time to read, talk to them about what they are reading
2. Create a reading page on my website to house the videos of adult and student book talks, links to book lists, and the link and the public Amazon wish list.
3. Survey former Stockbridge High School students to ask them about their college reading requirements. Use this information in the infographic or with students when I launch the independent reading portion of the class. Career and citizenship reading (nonrequired reading).

Timeframe: By August 30th (and do a video book talk as a demo)

Audience: Teachers

Do an "elevator talk" at the first staff meeting about the importance of reading and the ways we can help create a more vibrant reading community here at SHS.

- Ask teachers to volunteer to give videotaped book talks or share what they are reading on social media at #StockbridgeReads.
- Ask staff to donate used books to the media center.

4. Hand out "What I'm Reading" signs that staff can easily update, and invite staff to put them on their doors.

Timeframe: By August 30th

Intermediate Tactics:

Audience: English Department

1. Get the English department to hand out the infographic along with their syllabus.
2. Over the year, share the benefits of independent reading as a component of the English curriculum and how it has benefited my class.
3. Share how I manage and encourage independent reading, including how to encourage students to read texts of greater complexity.
4. Work together to develop a resource of videotaped book talks.
5. Include book talk as a component of the English department meeting.
6. Work with the town librarian to get every student a public library card and teach them how to check out books digitally and read them on their Chromebooks.

Timeframe: 2016–2017 school year and beyond

Audience: Administrators/SAEF grant/Book Love Foundation

1. Advocate for an adequate yearly book budget for books in the media center with my principal.
2. Apply for a Book Love grant for my classroom library.
3. Apply for an SAEF grant for books for my classroom library.
4. Videotape student testimony/book talks at the end of each semester to reinforce the benefits of independent reading programs.

Timeframe: Book Love grant due March 2017, 2016–2017 school year and beyond

Long-Term Tactics:

Goal: A budget for classroom libraries for every English teacher, and independent reading programs in every English class

Audience: Teachers/Administrators

- Demonstrate in my personal classroom the benefits for the reading program using data/videos to create an argument for a budget and implementation of independent reading programs.

Chapter 2

Working in Ways That Are Smart, Safe, Savvy, and Sustainable

The teachers you met in Chapter 1 are living demonstrations of the professionalism that is gained when teachers add advocacy knowledge to their pedagogical content knowledge. These teachers were immersed in the core ideas that underlie advocacy and organizing and have begun to see advocacy as an integral part of their teacher identity. They have put on their "advocacy caps" in order to help others in their community understand why and how they teach in the ways they do. In that chapter, we also shared some specific approaches that teachers, teacher educators, and teacher leaders might take to further their advocacy, including steps that lead to the creation of in-depth action plans.

At this point you may be wondering if these full-fledged plans are really necessary. Clearly, they require a lot of work, perhaps more than you think you can realistically take on. We certainly understand this reaction; it's one we've both asked ourselves and heard from other busy teachers and teacher educators over the years. Realistically, *Is advocacy still possible without all the steps that lead to a fully realized action plan?*

What we've come to learn through the lessons of community organizers and the work we've done with teachers and teacher educators is that while creating an action plan can certainly help effect change in a specific issue, teachers can take many smaller steps to chip away at the mischaracterizing narrative about teachers and literacy. What's most important in this work is to encourage teachers to integrate a commitment to advocacy work in their day-to-day teaching—a commitment that can take many forms. Our experience has shown us that teachers who create action plans make some stunning changes in their immediate environments, but that even a little, immersion in everyday advocacy leads teachers to change their mindset about their role as teachers. In other words, even though not every teacher we've worked with has created a fully realized action plan and followed through on all the steps, just being immersed in advocacy ideas helps these teachers see themselves differently.

So whether you incorporate full-fledged immersion in advocacy in your inter-actions with teachers or just dip a little bit into that work, we suggest that you, at the very least, emphasize with preservice and practicing teachers these important components of an everyday advocacy mindset: name and frame a specific issue that they care about; learn as much as they can about that issue; consider how that issue impacts their local work settings; define a clear goal of what they want to change or what they want others to understand differently; find a way of talking about that change in consideration of their audience; and come up with specific tactics that will help change that audience's mind. In other words, at the heart of everyday advocacy is a thoughtful, considered approach to making change with the acknowledgement that it will look different in different settings for different purposes.

In Part II of this book, we'll demonstrate those differences by sharing the voices of teachers across the country who are doing advocacy work, from full-fledged action plans that teachers have put into practice to more abbreviated versions from teachers who are using some of the approaches we offered in Chapter 1. These teacher vignettes confirm that teachers can indeed integrate this work into their already busy lives, that they find meaning in this work, and that the context in which they teach impacts their approach. As teacher educators and teacher leaders you may find inspiration in these stories and models of activism that you may want to share with the teachers with whom you work.

In Part III, we'll discuss ways that literacy teacher educators across the country are putting their advocacy knowledge into practice: from specific lessons in methods courses to more full-fledged assignments, workshops, and clubs. While the vignettes in that part don't represent all the possibilities for integrating everyday advocacy, we believe they offer a good range of options and, we hope, will inspire you to consider ways to include advocacy knowledge in your instruction.

But first, we want to dig in to some of the essential components of the mindset we consider vital for teachers to retain their professionalism in these complicated

Figure 2.1 Smart, Safe, Savvy, and Sustainable

Working in ways that are

Smart
Naming and knowing the issue

Learning what others think about the issue

Framing the issue in new ways

Understanding the context in which we work—including the students, families, and communities

Safe
Developing allies

Building awareness

Everyday Advocacy

Savvy
Moving from concern to action

Being strategic

Moving beyond a "tactics-only" approach

Sustainable

Making this a part of your day-to-day life

times. Passively receiving the latest mandates and feeling frustrated all the time doesn't lead to teacher satisfaction nor to long-term commitment to the profession. Railing against the machine, while immediately satisfying, can often threaten teachers' job security. We need a new model for a path in between—one that enables teachers to work to change the system but also to continue to succeed in it at the same time. With such a mindset, educators learn to work in ways that are *smart, safe, savvy,* and *sustainable,* as we show in Figure 2.1.

Working in Ways That Are Smart

The base of any kind of advocacy work is the importance of teachers being knowledgeable about their issue. The more teachers know about a particular issue (from choice reading to formative assessment to grammar in context to disciplinary writing), the more confident they will be when talking with others about the issue and the better able they will be to respond to questions, concerns, and critiques.

How do teachers gain this knowledge? First, teachers immerse themselves in what others have said about their issue by studying published research, examples from other teachers, blogs, proposed legislation, social media, and other published accounts. Learning through the expertise of others can help teachers increase their own knowledge base as they critically consider their own position on the issue, confirm their beliefs, and discover new ways of thinking and expressing their understanding.

One way to develop this knowledge draws upon what Winn, Graham, and Alfred (2019) refer to as a personalized syllabus, based on a self-audit of what you already know and what you still need to find out. Adapting their personalized syllabus to this context, teachers might begin with naming their issue, explaining why they are concerned about the issue, noting what they already know about the issue, and raising questions and concerns and noticing gaps in their knowledge. Teachers can then develop a list of resources that they want to investigate to learn more about the issue.

For example, Kris Gedeon, a high school teacher who has been committed to everyday advocacy for the past five years, recently began a project to create a library in her new school setting. The school, which is connected to a community college, has no library of its own and relies on the community college library, which is fairly light on novels in general and is particularly lacking in the kinds of multicultural and diverse young adult novels that Kris wants her students to read. To work in *smart* ways regarding this project, Kris developed a reading list for herself comprised of materials that covered 1) books, articles, and policy statements about library creation and sustainability, library–literacy connections, and the importance of access to diverse reading material; and 2) diverse novels, especially those written by people from groups to which she is less familiar. This reading list has helped Kris develop her expertise so that she can talk to others about libraries, and books within those libraries, with a new level of confidence.

A second way of developing this knowledge is more local, more focused on the specific context in which a teacher works. When teachers look carefully at their own students, focusing on learning and teaching in their own setting, they become teacher researchers. Teacher researchers create new knowledge by studying what their students tell them through surveys, interviews, and written documents and what they notice through careful classroom observations and the fieldnotes they keep in conjunction with those observations (Chiseri-Strater & Sunstein, 2009; Lytle & Cochran-Smith, 2009; Fleischer, et al., 2014). In their classroom studies, teacher researchers discover new ways of thinking that may confirm what they've read in outside resources, gaps between external research and their own, or new wonderings. Teachers who immerse themselves in classroom research develop marked levels of confidence, knowing that their study not only helps them understand their own classroom but can add to the ongoing public conversation surrounding an issue. Teacher researchers regularly tell us that they feel better able to talk to administrators, community members, and other decision-makers when they bring their own research findings into the conversation. (A long-term teacher research group that Cathy facilitates has come up with a motto that encapsulates that increased confidence: "Well, according to *my* research . . .")

For example, as Kris expands her knowledge about classroom libraries, she also draws on her experience as a teacher researcher. In addition to gaining knowledge from outside sources, she is focusing on her own students and their needs: interviewing them about their library usage, the kinds of books they read, and what appeals to them in choosing books; interviewing them about books they'd like to see in the library. She keeps field notes about her students' experiences with books. As she adds all this knowledge to the knowledge she's gained from external reading, she will be able to demonstrate to others a very deep expertise about books and libraries—knowledge that will help her to inform others, to speak articulately to their concerns, and to feel confident as she does so.

Working in Ways That Are Safe

Many teachers worry that advocacy work has the potential to put them at risk of repercussions, from being seen as "that person" whom colleagues avoid to losing their jobs. We know that these fears are real, that teachers who raise their voices can be seen as troublemakers or malcontents—especially if they try to do this work alone.

This is where some of the action principles mentioned in Chapter 1 come into play—in particular, the principle of building allies. Allies are vital for this work because they help teachers establish a network of people who serve as collaborators and sounding-boards and who help present a united front when a teacher suggests new ways of thinking about an issue or a drastic change in how teaching and learning are done in a school. Allies also can be those who have the ear of a decision-maker when a teacher does not, someone to whom the decision-maker might listen because of their status or position in a community.

Teachers can identify allies as they raise awareness about their issue of concern, usually in the proactive ways described in Chapter 1 (such as public events or newsletters that inform and educate parents and community members about why they are using a particular technique). Then high school teacher Jennifer Buehler, for example, created young adult book clubs for parents so they could understand what their teens were reading. Then high school teacher Sarah Andrew-Vaughan created a series of parent workshops on their own personal reading and writing histories so they could understand why she insists on choice in her classroom. lisa eddy created a YouTube channel for her classroom and videotaped writing workshop in action so parents could see how she teaches.

All of these approaches help educate and inform others about why these teachers teach in the ways they do. Quite often, those who become informed also become the teachers' strongest allies—they are able to talk to administrators, testify at school board meetings, and even reach out to legislators from their perspective. Raising awareness among others leads to allies. And allies lead to safety.

Working in Ways That Are Savvy

Teachers who are successful advocates share two important traits: they are both optimistic and planful.

Optimism may not be our first response when we consider this work. More often, our first response may be one of despair—despair at the situations that teachers face, at the dismissive reactions to teacher expertise, at the lack of respect for the work teachers do. But savvy teacher advocates work hard to put themselves into a different mindset—one that encourages them to recognize that change is possible. They believe, for example, the words of Grace Lee Boggs, the late Detroit organizer and activist, who told us that we have to move beyond the anger we often feel when we sense our voices are being dismissed from the public narrative about teaching and learning. "Just being angry, just being outraged," she reminds us, "does not constitute revolution" (Rosen, 2015, para. 25). Savvy teacher activists also believe the words of environmental activist Alex Steffen, when he exhorts us to move beyond the kind of crippling pessimism we feel when we fear that there's nothing we can do to create change. "Optimism," he counters, "is a political act. Those who benefit from the status quo are perfectly happy for us to think nothing is going to get any better. In fact, these days, cynicism is obedience" (Belden, 2010, para. 2). For both Boggs and Steffen as well as for many others who are committed to activism, advocacy begins in the mindset that we can indeed make a difference. Savvy teacher advocates, in other words, begin with the understanding that we can indeed do something beyond feeling angry, beyond feeling defeated.

This leads to the second component of a savvy mindset: becoming planful. A planful approach to advocacy is something that teachers can learn through many of the strategies mentioned in Chapter 1, through the examples we offer of teacher-led advocacy in the chapters that follow, or though the kinds of advocacy training offered by organizations like the Midwest Academy (http://www.midwestacademy.com/training/organizing-social-change/), Beautiful Trouble (https://beautifultrouble .org/), re:power (formerly Wellstone Action) (https://repower.org/), or Resistance School (https://www.resistanceschool.com/#resistschool). We know that, for many of us, this kind of thoughtful, slow-paced advocacy does not come naturally. Too often, our first tendency is to move straight to tactics without always strategically considering the vital connections between message and audience that we explained in greater detail in Chapter 1. The specific moves we suggest in Chapter 1 are a part of being deliberately planful: moves like re-formulating a bigger concern into something that is both contextual and manageable; identifying the decision-makers and audiences for our work; packaging that message in a way that makes sense for different audiences; and identifying the action steps that can speak to each of those audiences. Again, as we explained in the Chapter 1, there are specific strategies to each of these moves, strategies that are learnable and do-able.

We see this optimism and this planfulness at work in teachers we've worked with and whom we would consider savvy: teachers who look ahead and deliberately create connections with others to develop allies; teachers who work from multiple perspectives to bring in different audiences; teachers who see how each step can lead to the next one but allow for flexibility and serendipity; teachers who are prepared when those just-right moments for outreach crop up; teachers who refuse to be discouraged when a plan falls through and instead search for a different way in.

Working in Ways That Are Sustainable

Teachers cannot be advocates 24/7. They have to teach their classes, plan curricula and lessons, grade papers, meet with parents, serve as club advisors, attend meetings . . . the list goes on and on. But, as high school English teacher Alaina Feliks (whose plan you read in Chapter 1 and whose fuller story you'll encounter in Chapter 3) tells us, advocacy work can energize your teaching. For teachers like Alaina, the question becomes how to make this work sustainable—how to make it a part of what they do on a regular basis rather than just another add-on to an already too-busy schedule. The essence of this mindset toward sustainability is in teachers recognizing advocacy as part of their professional identity, what we refer to throughout this book as advocacy knowledge—akin to knowledge of content and knowledge of pedagogy. Sustainability, then, begins with the ways literacy educators introduce advocacy to preservice teachers and support it through teachers' ongoing professional learning experiences.

How do teachers sustain advocacy? Our experience suggests that it begins when teachers find collaborators and partners in this work. When they have others with whom they can share the load, talk about next steps, and celebrate successes, they are more likely to keep going—both as teachers and as teachers trying to make change. Sometimes those others are colleagues in the school or district—local others who are concerned about the same issues and who are working together to enact change. Sometimes those others are part of an advocacy group outside of a single school setting—teachers who may share a commitment to advocacy but whose contexts are different. In Figure 2.2, Melissa Brooks-Yip describes the sustainability of a professional community. And sometimes those others are the professional organizations to which teachers belong, organizations that offer support through conferences, web-seminars, publications, and social media. Each of these levels offers a different kind of support, but at their essence, they help teachers know that they are not alone in this work.

A second factor in the sustainability mindset is the understanding that change takes time. In other words, when teachers believe their advocacy project has to result in large-scale change in order to be deemed successful, they may feel frustrated when that change is not achieved immediately or when the small changes they do achieve seem insignificant. Teachers who are involved in advocacy for the long haul see it differently. Alaina Feliks, for example, suggests that sustainability begins by first seeing the whole picture—the change you desire and can imagine—then focusing on a few steps at a time. When you do one or two actions a year, she says, you begin to build momentum—with other teachers, with administrators, and even with the community. That momentum, she says, gives her the enthusiasm to continue.

One way teachers can remind themselves about the small steps is to develop an advocacy calendar, a listing of one action—however small—they want to do each week, each month, or each semester. Naming that action, recognizing the impact of that action, and using that action to build to the next step can help teachers see how advocacy can become an innate part of their professional lives—something that can energize them.

Figure 2.2 Working in Ways That Are Sustainable Through Professional Learning

Melissa Brooks-Yip, literacy coordinator for a large countywide school district, explains her role in advocating for teachers in smart, safe, savvy, and sustainable ways:

> For me, the heart of advocacy is guiding teachers to put themselves at the center of their own learning about their teaching practice. To advocate for teachers as professionals, dedicated to perfecting their craft, I began the Study of Early Literacy (SOEL) professional learning network in 2013. In SOEL, we focus on strengthening the pedagogical content knowledge of teachers through continued study, experiences, collaboration, and Teacher Action Research. We de-emphasize reliance on and expectations of purchased programs because we know it is *teachers who teach*.

I sustain SOEL by staying true to advocating for teacher learning through:

- **Coordinating ongoing, high quality professional resources and experiences—** Throughout our six meetings per year, we read professional texts, learn from expert speakers, and together visit schools to observe instructional practices.

- **Creating a culture of learning and sharing together—**We acknowledge our strengths and our challenges in the classroom and, through teacher presentations, discussions, and co-planning, we learn from each other to grow our practices.

- **The Teacher Action Research Cycle—**Each year, teachers develop their own question based on a problem of practice they identify for themselves. By trying new instructional practices learned in SOEL with students, and following the data collected, teachers intentionally improve their practice for student achievement.

- **Being transparent about and sharing our learning—**SOEL is a community of teachers who come together for several meetings during the school year, and sometimes for a period of years. To foster future participation and share our culture of learning, we are transparent about our activities in SOEL by sharing widely on social media, by having standing invitations to administrators to join us in meetings, and by hosting the meetings in schools, giving teachers a chance to showcase their strengths in instruction and student learning.

What's Next

Even if teachers don't create full-fledged action plans, adopting an advocacy mind-set is the start toward creating change and changing the public narrative about teachers and teaching. But what does it actually look like when teachers work in ways that are smart, safe, savvy, and sustainable? In the next section of the book we introduce you to classroom teachers for whom advocacy has made a difference. And while their settings and approaches to advocacy differ, they have much in common. As you read, we invite you to immerse yourselves in their worlds and think about how their approaches might impact your own.

References

Belden, D. (2010). The bright green city: Alex Steffen's optimistic environmentalism. *Tikkun Daily.* April 6, 2010. https://www.tikkun.org/tikkundaily/2010/04/06/the-bright-green-city-alex-steffens-optimistic-environmentalism/

Chiseri-Strater, E., & Sunstein B. (2009). *What works? A practical guide to teacher research.* Portsmouth, NH: Heinemann.

Fleischer, C., Daniel, E., eddy, l., Gedeon, K., DeYoung Kander, J., Kangas, D., & Guinot Varty, N. (2014). Teacher researchers as local agents of change: Exploding the myth of the bad teacher. *Language Arts Journal of Michigan, 29*(2), 259–275. . doi.org/10.9707/2168-149X.2012

Lytle, S. & Cochran-Smith, M. (2009). *Inquiry as stance: Practitioner research for the next generation.* New York, NY: Teachers College Press.

Rosen, Z. (Producer). (2015, Oct 5). *Remembering Grace Lee Boggs* [Audio NPR story and transcript]. Retrieved from http://michiganradio.org/post/remembering-detroits-grace-lee-boggs

Shulman, Lee S. (1986). "Those who understand: Knowledge growth in teaching. *Educational Researcher, 15*(2), 4–14.

Winn, M., Graham, H., & Alfred, R. (2019). *Restorative justice in the English classroom.* Urbana, IL: NCTE.

PART II

Centering Advocacy in Secondary ELA Instruction

We are obviously pretty big proponents of the ideas described in Part I of the book. And while we—Cathy and Antero—could continue to espouse the goals of everyday advocacy and provide you with a lengthy pep talk throughout the rest of this volume, Part II instead brings to light the specific ways that teachers already are doing the work of everyday advocacy every day. If you read the opening chapters of this book with a "Yes, but . . ." lingering in your head as you imagined the logistics in your own context, these next next six chapters highlight a handful of teachers who have been in the same place that you have and whose lessons, ideas, and ingenuity have taught us so much.

In the first section of this book, we introduced and reviewed the key principles of everyday advocacy and dug into some of the key steps you'll need to take—as a learner, as a teacher, as a teacher educator, as a leader, as a critical advocate. We've also suggested that advocacy is indeed contextual: not all advocacy approaches look the same due to varying comfort levels and differences in circumstances. In this part of the book, we illustrate how context matters as we share the diverse and creative voices of friends and leaders in literacy instruction. We hope that these stories, along with our brief opening comments of acknowledgement and context and brief closing comments on key considerations inspire and challenge you in your own work.

Merely a Starting Place

It is important to note that, while some of the teacher voices in this section specifically name aspects of Everyday Advocacy within their chapters, the majority of these teachers highlight their decisions and instructional moves without referring to the four S's that frame the principles of this book (working in ways that are smart, savvy, safe, and sustainable). In fact, only Alaina Feliks (Chapter 3) and Rick Joseph (Chapter 7) participated in the Everyday Advocacy summer workshops that Cathy facilitates. The rest of the contributors were solicited based on our personal knowledge of the powerful leadership, ingenuity, and commitment to the literary lives of young people that they represent. There are countless other teachers out there who also are engaged in this powerful work (and we imagine you, reading this book, might count yourselves among them or may know of others who are advocating as part of their everyday lives as teachers). And so, these voices are intended only to offer a starting place for your own journey as an advocate for our profession and for our students. Whether you adapt a particular approach, find inspiration in the ways teachers work within the complicated systems of schooling, or refer to these examples to bolster your rationale for forms of advocacy within your school site, use these brief chapters as a launching point for your own work—as a teacher, a teacher leader, or a teacher educator.

Just as the cases we included are only a preliminary smattering of the topics around which advocacy is shaped, so too do they only hint at the variety of possible advocacy-driven actions. The approaches, designs, and challenges that these teachers face must inherently change from one year to the next; the world does not sit by idly waiting for advocacy to address a given need.

In the early pages of this book, we described the conundrum of shifting demands on the teaching profession today. Today, it is not enough for teachers to build solely on pedagogical content knowledge. Rather, we must also include *advocacy knowledge* as a core component of the work we do in classrooms, in our professional lives outside of classrooms, and even in the informal settings in which we describe the work we do as teachers—at social gatherings, through our own political and cultural participation, etc. Viewed as a necessary aspect of what teachers must do today—what *you* must do today—Lee Shulman's (1986) now decades-old definition of pedagogical content knowledge actually offers some clear descriptions of how advocacy functioned as an embodied form of knowledge with and for teachers; he explains that this form of knowledge "goes beyond knowledge of subject matter per se to the dimension of subject matter knowledge for teaching" (Shulman, 1986, p. 9). This synthesis—knowing about something as well as knowing what might be most salient for in instruction and learning—is exactly what is at the heart of the advocacy knowledge on display within the chapters in this section. In your own practice, it is not enough to know the frames and principles of Everyday Advocacy. Rather, we think this knowledge also includes the tacit skills of understanding how to apply advocacy-driven approaches to schooling—advocacy knowledge—to your specific school and classroom contexts.

This knowledge is hard won through the crucible of time, experience, and humility. While we hope you gain insight from the lessons of the other teachers whose voices lift this section of the book, this book-knowledge is only one dimension of how you grow as an advocate for the literacy needs in your classroom. Like a muscle that strengthens over time with consistent use, your growth as an advocate occurs only when you actually practice advocating! Similarly, just as muscle might strengthen under the resistance of weight, your advocacy knowledge, too, will improve because of the challenges you will inevitably face. And the good news is, you don't have to advocate alone and you don't have to be a sole trailblazer.

Advocating Alongside

The collective memory of your school and its surrounding community likely exceeds the years you have been teaching and working within your current placement. Even if you were born and raised in the surrounding area, histories are myriad and they are lengthy. In light of this, consider: who else might shed insights and potentially work as a partner in the thinking, planning, and enacting of your everyday advocacy efforts? We want to be clear that these partners do not necessarily always need to be teachers. Yes, administrators often have commitments aligned to the literary lives of young people. Even if your theories of change diverge, consider when and where bringing in administrators, instructional coaches, and other adult staff might help advance your work. Similarly, parents—a huge and critical component to your success in the classroom—should be trusted participants in your work. And finally, though omnipresent in nearly every aspect of the work we do, students are often given short shrift when we consider with whom we might partner and how. Contrary to mainstream narratives of aloof and disengaged youth, students care *deeply* about their opportunities to learn and to improve the conditions of schooling and literacy development for themselves and for their peers.

As an additional note on working alongside—and in the best interests of—students, the power dynamics in schools are intentionally set up to allow you, as a salary-drawing adult, to wield more power than your students. Bringing in students as respected partners in the advocacy efforts you are leading will require acknowledging this power and approaching your students with an authentic humility that allows you to see and incorporate the full humanity of the students you are working for and with.

Honoring the Time and Scale of Advocacy

Alongside the partnering dimensions of this work, another challenge we hear from teachers interested in everyday advocacy is *making* the time. For many of us, our days begin long before school starts and continue for hours after the bell rings (often with little downtime to catch our breath). You may be reading this wondering if even *finding* the time for another aspect of teaching is possible. The ways we describe time emphasize it as a precious commodity to make, to find, and to cherish. It is because of this very legitimate feeling of too-muchness that we highlight these particular teacher stories in this section of the book. To be clear, the constant pull on our time from various directions is a factor of teaching that we think requires vigilance and advocacy as a topic in and of itself; we think nearly every teacher is intimately familiar with feeling overwhelmed.

As you imagine how these chapters may reflect the interests and needs of your own school setting, we encourage you to consider the frames of proximal and distal outcomes of interventions, policies, and your own advocacy efforts. For example, long-term and schoolwide investment in an independent reading assessment program may have research-backed evidence espousing the merits for increasing Lexile level comprehension for students. This distal outcome, however, may not reflect how student reading interest and passion are potentially thwarted by a limited selection of books; the program at the school Antero taught at depended on students reading within a narrowly-defined range of books. Many students were left with book choices that did not reflect their interests and that felt humiliating to read in class based on the book's childish designs and large font design. When our efforts to address literacy instruction in schools focus solely on short-term or solely on long-term change, unintended effects may result. What may feel like a commitment to equity and addressing a literacy achievement gap—as in the case at Antero's school—can actually become a demoralizing form of high-stakes assessment that ultimately frames reading as required drudgery.

Consider how the chapters that follow attend to the proximal and the distal outcomes related to advocacy as you imagine the proactive steps you will take in your own design. When Rick Joseph describes an intersectional book-pass activity, he frames this as an in-the-moment activity that is aligned to his instructional goals and that also helps shape long-term interest and expansive worldviews. Rick's example (and others you'll soon read) are contextual examples of teachers actively ensuring that their classrooms are moving toward justice, one change at a time.

Sustainable Possibilities

If you've read this far, then by now you surely have ideas of advocacy swimming in your head, itching to be enacted. As you listen to the polyphony of voices engaged in everyday advocacy in the following chapters, consider how you can intentionally frame the work you are doing as advocacy and also how you *feel* about this advocacy-focused educator identity. Like Rosenblatt's (1978) classic framing of reader response theory, we invite you to be in dialogue with the contributions in this section. How would you build on Kristen Strom's (Chapter 5) reflections on utilizing social media as a tool for advocacy? Similarly, what would it mean to be the sixth member of the writing group described in Chapter 6? Even as we highlight these authors, we hope you will read them and their work less as paragons of advocacy and more as possible guidelines or ideas for you to consider regarding what is manageable for you where you are in your career now. We reached out to friends and colleagues whom we've had the privilege to learn from and asked them to write their chapters for *you*—a committed English educator or teacher leader.

In this spirit, we end each of these chapters with our own takeaways of what we've learned as we discussed and learned from reviewing the chapters our colleagues wrote. We intentionally highlight nuances within these chapters and offer prompts you can use to expand your thinking around engaging in advocacy at your school. We now step back and give way to the voices of teachers.

Reference

Rosenblatt, L. M. (1978). *The reader, the text, the poem: The transactional theory of the literary work*. Carbondale: Southern Illinois University Press.

Shulman, L. S. (1986). Those who understand: Knowledge growth in teaching. *Educational Researcher, 15*(2), 4–14.

Chapter 3

Creating a Buzz About Reading

Growing Mindsets

Alaina Feliks

Alaina Feliks now teaches English at Skyline High School in Ann Arbor, Michigan. At the time she participated in the Everyday Advocacy workshop, she was teaching at Stockbridge High School, also in Michigan. Here, Alaina chronicles her journey toward changing the narrative around reading in her small community, including the ways she implemented that plan over the course of several years.

When I started my advocacy project, I had been teaching English for 14 years in a small, rural district in Michigan. The population there is over-whelmingly white. Over 40% of students in the district are considered economically disadvantaged. The town has just one small library branch. Students live miles away from well-stocked libraries and bookstores, and many families simply don't have books in their homes. Additionally, the district no longer employs certified school librarians to manage library collections or to work with young readers.

There is ample research on the academic and lifelong benefits of reading. However, many of my students simply did not identify themselves as readers. Many Stockbridge students pursue technical careers, and, until they met me, they didn't see how reading was relevant to them. Additionally, Stockbridge students live in a very homogenous community. I looked at research on how reading promotes empathy and realized that pushing a reading agenda might be a good way to help students imagine perspectives that are far different from their own.

Another layer to my story is that, at the time I started my advocacy project, the school was consolidating and transitioning to a 7–12 building, going through major renovations, and experiencing administrative turnover. Although it may be counterintuitive, I found that this was the perfect time to advocate for changes in the reading culture of the school.

Through my participation in Cathy Fleischer's advocacy workshop, I developed a plan to change the narrative around reading in the school. I wanted to generate more buzz around reading, and I also wanted to make sure students had access to books from diverse perspectives on high-interest topics. In 2016, the first year of the project, I started by distilling some of my research on reading into a simple infographic, and I created a Stockbridge Reads website to connect students and community members with book recommendations. Then, I worked to develop allies. I approached my English department with my ideas, and every member of my department agreed to help in some way. (See Figures 3.1 and 3.2.) Some distributed the infographic with their syllabus, and some added to my project with ideas of their own, including having a librarian from the local library visit our classes to help students get library cards and learn to access materials. We also began collaborating on how to engage our students in reading through independent reading programs in our classes. We talked more about the books we and our students were reading and, together, developed more ways to hook young people on reading, from daily book talks to videos to images that we displayed in our classroom that celebrated students' reading accomplishments. We used the website I created to publish students' book talk videos and celebrate students' reading.

No amount of buzz about reading can really work if students don't have access to interesting books. Another important thread of this advocacy work was to secure funding for books. Research suggests that having access to books within the classroom is extremely impactful on a student's reading, and in a 7–12 school, there is a very wide range of reading levels and interests.

In the first year of the project, I focused on obtaining books for the school library by creating a DonorsChoose project, an Amazon wish list, and simply asking for donations of gently used books from staff and community members (see Figure 3.3). I shared these requests with the community through the Stockbridge Reads website and teachers in the English department shared the requests through their parent communications. Additionally, the school newspaper ran a story about our campaign. That year, the school administration agreed to budget an annual allowance for new books for the library. That, along with the fully funded DonorsChoose project and other donations, meant that the library got hundreds of new titles that year.

At the end of the first year of the project, I turned my focus to funding for classroom libraries. In the transition to a 7–12 building, we discovered that there were still many copies of books in the old middle school library. With another colleague, I spent hours sorting through that collection and moving books from the middle school to the high school. As an English department, we also applied for and received a grant to fund 50 new books for each 7–12 English teacher to begin or supplement our classroom libraries. The next year, our department was under curriculum review and was due for new materials. We advocated for and received a yearly budget for classroom libraries for each ELA classroom.

I also tried to expand this buzz about reading outside of the English department. I presented my infographic at a staff meeting and invited adults in the building to do video book talks about books that they loved. In the second year of the project, I made "what I'm reading" wall hangers for every staff member in our building so that adults' reading lives would be more visible to students and to promote conversations about books.

I don't want to make this sound too easy. There were many frustrations and setbacks along the way. For instance, between year one and two of my project, as the school was undergoing renovations in its move to a 7–12 building, hundreds of books from the school library were thrown out without consulting anyone from the English department. After some investigating, I discovered that the discarded books were still being stored in the old middle school building, and I spent hours, tearfully and angrily, going through the boxes to salvage books for classroom libraries, including books that we had just purchased with DonorsChoose funds the previous year. Even more challenging, of course, is that it is not so easy to change people's attitudes about anything, including reading. Shifting students' ideas about themselves as readers is an ongoing process that takes time and a tremendous amount of effort. It takes persistence from all involved and faith in little steps forward.

Even though the steps were small and incremental, I can say that three years after I developed my idea in Cathy's advocacy workshop, Stockbridge did show some real changes around reading. The school is filled with more diverse, high-interest books, and every teacher in the English department has committed, at some level, to incorporating choice, independent reading as part of their course. I took a job in another district, but the work has continued without me. My former colleagues took over the website and continue to grow classroom libraries and develop robust independent reading programs. My biggest source of pride came from a conversation I had with one of my colleagues in which she told me that when she saw the advocacy work that I was doing, she realized her own power to make change in the school. Since then, she has started a faculty book club and sponsored the school's first Gay Straight Alliance as well as taking the lead on advocating for real reading.

Overall, what I want to tell teachers is that no change will happen all at once. We are all busy and can only work on our advocacy in small chunks. My project took several years and is still ongoing. However, taking one small step at a time will produce results. I learned to celebrate small victories and found that becoming engaged in trying to change one aspect of my school invigorated me and helped fuel my love of teaching.

Figure 3.1 Email to Teacher Colleagues

This is a copy of the first email I sent to my English department to enlist their help with the project.

Hi all,

I hope you have been having a wonderful summer! These last few weeks are always so bittersweet to me: I'm sad to see summer end but so excited to get back to work. Seeing J_____ at school this week and talking shop sort of tipped me to the excited side, so I am going to unleash some of that on you all right now!

I wanted to share with you what I have been working on this summer. One small thing that I would like to work on this school year is to promote more of a reading culture in our school and community. Here are some ideas I have for doing this:

1. I created a simple infographic to share with parents about the importance of reading and ways they can help support the library. It is the first page on the Stockbridge Reads website. If you have any suggestion for it, let me know. If I printed it out would you be willing to hand it out along with your syllabus?

2. *I created a Weebly page called Stockbridge Reads (stockbridgereads.weebly.com). It is pretty rough, and I hope to continue to evolve it, but right now it has resources for finding good books, getting e-books, and ways people can support the high school library. I'm hoping this is something we can all collaborate on: each of us can add resources and make it more robust. Any help you can give with resources or design would be much appreciated.*

3. *I am going to try to promote reading through social media with #StockbridgeReads. If you are on social media, I would love it if you would help me by posting selfies of you with your current book. I also plan to post pictures of students reading.*

4. *I set up a YouTube channel for Stockbridge Reads that can be a resource for book talks for all of us. Pam and I were talking about how it is impossible for us, individually, to read everything that kids might be interested in, but I thought if we sort of pooled our resources, we could create a good database of video book talks, which can be tagged with the type of book, who did the book talk, etc. I also plan to have students do them. The goal is to have lots of different people talking about lots of different books. I posted one, which is pretty rough, but I think that hopefully shows that they don't have to be perfect.*

5. *I created a GoFundMe site for the library as well. That link will also be on the website.*

So, for YouTube and Weebly, I created a new gmail account called StockbridgeReads. If you log into Google as Stockbridge Reads, you can add videos to the YouTube channel and access the Weebly site.

Let me know if you have any questions or suggestions for any of this!

The website I created can be found at http://stockbridgereads.weebly.com/

Figure 3.2 Note to Teacher Colleagues

Stockbridge Reads!

As I mentioned at the first staff meeting, studies show that regular pleasure reading gives students a **four times greater** academic advantage than having a parent with an advanced degree. Reading matters to our students and our school.

We can make a difference in students' academic and personal success **this year** by creating more of a buzz around reading in this school. Here are some ways you can help:

- Hang an **infographic** in your room about reading. See me—I have plenty.
- Take a **selfie** with one of your favorite books or a book you read this summer and post it to social media with the hashtag Stockbridge Reads.
- Record a short video book talk to share a favorite book on the Stockbridge Reads YouTube channel. I'll take a video of you before or after school, or if you want to do it yourself, share it with me.
- Talk to students about what you are reading. We are working on **new room signs** to help start the conversation.
- Donate used books to the media center and share the GoFundMe website with parents and community members.
- Visit the Stockbridge Reads website for more information and links to great reading resources!
- Do you have other ideas? Share them!

Figure 3.3 Screenshot From My Fully Funded DonorsChoose Project for Classroom Library Books

I was thrilled that some parents and former students donated.

$591 GOAL

HOORAY! THIS PROJECT IS FULLY FUNDED

They are curious and smart and need access to resources to help their dreams become reality. One of the best things my students can do to help them prepare for the demands of college and the world beyond our small town is to become committed, voracious readers.

My Project

Recent studies show that reading for pleasure is one of the most important factors in students' academic success.

> *The effect of regular pleasure reading was four times greater than the advantage students gained from having a parent with an advanced degree.*

Children who choose what they read tend to read more, to be more motivated, show stronger literacy and language skills and they tend to score better in math.

In order to promote a culture of reading, I need new books for my classroom library. Having books in the classroom is proven to increase student reading. In fact, one study showed that students with a classroom library read 60% more than a control group.

More than a third of students from low-income households

14 donors have given to this project.

This project will reach 100 students.

Stockbridge, MI   Grades 9–12

More than a third of students from low-income households

Literacy   Literature & Writing

SHARE MS. FELIKS'S PROJECT

Figure 3.4 Door Hangers
I designed this as the door hanger and offered it to every staff member in
the building.

I'M READING...

SEEK THE LOFTY BY READING, HEARING AND
SEEING GREAT WORK AT SOME MOMENT
EVERY DAY--- THORNTON WILDER

What We Noticed as We Read This Chapter

Kicking off the contributor chapters, Alaina Feliks' chapter explores the highs and lows of implementing an advocacy plan within her local school community. Like several other chapters in this section, Alaina's narrative illuminates some common themes of designing, preparing for, and enacting everyday advocacy.

- *The context of your advocacy project matters.* Alaina describes the place—a small, rural district in Michigan with a high number of students designated "economically disadvantaged." Alaina's decade-and-a-half of teaching experience within this district allows her to feel confident about her grasp of the literacy resources within the community, the varied school transitions, and the myriad structural changes that her students experienced during the period that she focused on expanding the reading opportunities for students.

  Questions to consider: What is your context for this work? What are some important considerations of context in terms of your own approaches to advocacy?

- *The importance of naming a goal that appeals to a broad audience.* Alaina states a broad goal early on in her chapter; her focus of trying to "generate more buzz around reading" is one that multiple stakeholders would be interested in and that allowed her efforts to center on book access and the needs of the diverse learners she serves. To do so, she relies on bodies of research, as well as communicative practices, to build awareness and action around her goals. For example, she describes how she creates infographics and a website dedicated to improving reading opportunities. These multimodal products were then shared with other teachers, which led to collaboration. Writing—as a central tool in the hands of everyday advocates—builds allyship, conveys expertise, and offers specific instructions for how others can support your work. As Alaina describes what transpired over her months of effort, we notice where the effects of her work was felt: in collaboration with colleagues, as a prolonged impact on students, and as structural goals for the school and the community.

Questions to consider: How might you develop allies as you do this work? What might you share with them (research, products you create) to help create shared knowledge?

- *Setbacks are a part of the advocacy process.* Alaina also didn't shy away from the setbacks that she faced during her advocacy efforts. Her description of the frustration in finding (and trying to salvage) books that were being thrown out reminds us that advocacy in the real world doesn't always go as smoothly as we may hope, despite our best laid plans. In light of this, we encourage readers to heed her advice to focus *persistently* on the broader goals of advocacy despite moments when you might falter. Alaina's persistence is focused primarily on shifting the beliefs and attitudes of students as readers. However, her chapter also speaks to the work required to shift what *adults* believe about kids, literacy practices, and how schools and communities sustain reading engagement.

  Questions to consider: What ways of thinking might help you face setbacks in your advocacy work? How might you create networks of support to help you on those occasions when the work doesn't go smoothly?

- *Advocacy takes time.* Throughout this chapter, the sense of *time* is ever present. Advocacy takes a lot of it. That sense of growth (and the patience it requires) can be rewarding. But we want readers to note that this "patient impatience" is a key characteristic we must become skilled at if we are to successfully engage in field-based advocacy.

  Questions to consider: How might you find the time to take on the work of advocacy? What small steps can you take on at first?

We think this chapter is a powerful reflection of a savvy, well-designed plan that moved alongside the needs of students. Alaina built on her expertise as an educator—knowing how to communicate with colleagues and how to instruct students in ways that undergird a commitment to literacy.

Chapter 4

Advocating for a Third Space

Shifting the Narrative Surrounding Secondary School Writing Centers

Jeffrey Austin

Jeff Austin focuses this piece on his experiences as a high school writing center director who is committed to issues of equity and justice. As he works to shift traditional understandings of the purpose of writing centers, he relies on advocacy measures—from developing allies to strategically shifting the conversation. He also invites us to see how students, too, become advocates for new ways of defining the purpose of writing center work.

Skyline High School in Ann Arbor, Michigan, is among the schools regularly featured on "best of" lists, and as the English Department Chair, Instructional Coach, and Writing Center Director there, I feel there is a ton to be proud of. The teachers are legitimately world-class, the resources are incredible, especially compared with those in my previous schools, and the students are thoughtful and empathetic. It's easy to be drawn to Skyline whether you are a teacher, parent, or student.

But while Skyline is generally a high-achieving school in a well-resourced district, a closer look at student achievement data during my first year at Skyline in 2011 revealed significantly disproportionate learning outcomes in literacy and writing among certain groups of students, including students of color, students with socioeconomic disadvantages, and students with special education plans. As a result of this data, the State of

Michigan designated Skyline, along with many other Ann Arbor schools, as a "focus school" because of the significant equity gaps. While issues of equity and inclusion have always been at the forefront of my classroom pedagogy, I thought more about how the systemic inequities being confronted at Skyline required systemic solutions that could usher in significant shifts in mindsets and practices, particularly around literacy.

How could I, as an English teacher wanting to create a more equitable and just school, contribute to the call to normalize high expectations and achievment for all students? How could I respond to a systemwide urgency to implement programs and initiatives capable of changing the disproportional practices leading to these inequitable outcomes? Heeding the call for action, I proposed opening the Skyline Writing Center, a student-led, student-centered program that provides high-quality writing support to students in a physical writing center, in classrooms, and online while also functioning as a literacy hub within the school. I pitched the Writing Center as a "third space," focusing less on traditional markers of academic success, like grades, and more on building the literacy identities necessary for students' sustained personal and academic growth. A group of decidated students and I rooted much of our work in anti-racist, anti-bias approaches to teaching and learning that honor and value all literacies and languages, even if those approaches aren't always valued academically.

While vital youth-driven third spaces exist throughout the Ann Arbor community, building and sustaining a student-led, student-centered third space within the context of a traditional secondary school presented challenges. Among the most substantial obstacles were skepticism of youth-driven spaces and, sadly, a distrust of students. Despite the documented benefits of peer writing centers and their work, many adults—teachers, administrators, parents—simply did not believe that students could provide effective literacy support for other students. In other words, many adults believed that a writing center would change, and perhaps even supplant, teacher roles and practices. But at the center of our work was this idea: peer tutoring can't ever be a substitute for classroom teaching and learning, but peer writing centers can positively impact classroom practices, which is important if inequitable outcomes are the result of inequitable practices.

As the Writing Center has become more ingrained in the school culture through time and our advocacy efforts, we have seen a shift in perception: our usage has increased (since the Writing Center opened in 2012, tutors have completed more than 8,500 sessions); more teachers are making time for the prewriting and revising components of the writing process; some teachers are rethinking grading and assessment practices, especially in our English courses; and there is a greater trust that peer tutors can be an important part of students' writing experiences. In other words, our experience shows that peer writing centers can be built to disrupt traditional power hierarchies that sometimes exist among students and teachers as well as shift the discussion about what counts as literacy and literacy instruction. Our students not only helped shift the focus from product to process, but also worked to build relationships with their peers by giving them the individualized support and attention they needed. Their vision was about valuing their classmates' stories more than the "stuff" of school, like grades, rubrics, and test scores. Without prioritizing stories over stuff, we knew that we were simply going to recreate the power dynamics that we were working against.

We also recognized that if we wanted to shift the narrative surrounding writing centers, to show that our Writing Center wasn't about editing writing but rather about inspiring it, we would have to prove to our community that students could do this work with other students. Three moves were crucial to shifting that narrative and showing our community that youth-driven literacy spaces could be successful: First, we had to set clear, attainable, short-, medium-, and long-term goals to increase student achievement; second, we had to help students adopt positive writerly identities that could be tracked by collectable quantitative and qualitative data; and third, we had to leverage relationships with early adopters on our teaching staff, who believed in the writing center model and who would use the Writing Center in beta form, to help us gather data and improve our practices. All three of these moves required advocacy on the part of the core group of tutors, as they became the face of the Writing Center.

Despite the substantial growth of secondary school writing centers over the past decade, many internal and external stakeholders misunderstood the goals of the Writing Center, seeing tutors as teacher proxies meant to replicate the strictures and structures of the classroom in one-on-one tutoring. Our tutors experienced frustration as others—other students, other teachers, other administrators—at times told a very different version of our story to themselves and to others. We needed to tell our own story, but that meant we had to consider both our core beliefs and the data we collected, to frame a two-part, intertwined narrative that was true to ourselves and easy to articulate to those outside of the program: how the Writing Center's social justice lens could lead to systemic and meaningful change in students' literacy and how tutors could play a significant role in improving students' literacy.

Over the next two years, we developed a social justice and equity statement that forced us to examine our implicit biases and the systemic inequities around us and to develop a plan to work against both. One result of that statement was to work actively to recruit more tutors that represented the diversity of our school population. Representation is important, and because we believe that everyone's a writer, we wanted to make sure all students could see themselves in the Center. Out of our social justice and equity statement, the goal of reducing educational inequity by changing practices around writing and literacy began to emerge, as did four core beliefs that have come to give shape to the program: 1) honoring growth mindset and the belief that everyone can and wants to learn 2) presuming students' competence and multiplying their funds of knowledge, 3) sharing vulnerability, and 4) participating in literacy-based community outreach. Based on substantial research and years of thoughtful discussion, these goals became cornerstones of our attempts to inspire students to build writerly identities and to share our stories with our community.

Cementing our equity plan, developing our core values, and building a tutor training program rooted in anti-racist, anti-bias frameworks, we have had an impact on who visits the Writing Center. Half the students who use the Skyline Writing Center services are minoritized students, and 70 percent of these students are freshmen and sophomores. Based on the feedback we collect at the end of every tutoring session, minoritized students say they feel comfortable working with our tutors, that their voice is respected, and they are more confident in their skills and abilities. Ninety-nine percent say the Writing Center helped them significantly.

Learning to tell our story helped students consider how to talk effectively to their parents, friends, teachers, administrators, and outside partners about our mission and vision and gave them the confidence to do so. We thought carefully about how to shape our message, where to share it, and what form or genre that messaging might take. Students have helped build our website (skylinewritingcenter.org), they have made videos to share our program's goals and accomplishments with internal and external audiences (like the example on the homepage of the website), they write blogs about important issues of educational equity (skylinewritingcenter.org/blog), and they participate in education-related Twitter chats.

In addition, Skyline tutors have presented at local, regional, and national conferences; they've helped a number of other schools develop their writing centers as mentors; and they're even starting plans to work with local elementary schools in more targeted ways during the school day.

As a student-led, student-centered space, tutors needed to be the faces and voices of our program on social media and in person, but it was important to help them learn how to be advocates, a role they're not often asked to play in school. Getting students to consider genre, audience, and purpose in stakeholder communication took some practice. It required talking about our mission in someone else's language, that is, language that would be meaningful to others. For instance, some of our posts—while shared widely—are really targeted directly for school or district leaders, such as our superintendent. If they like or retweet us, we know we've been successful at messaging and getting them to notice and amplify our work, regardless of how many other interactions we get.

To do this sophisticated kind of advocacy, students need not only to have a deep understanding of our purpose and our methods but also to be able to use Writing Center data to speak meaningfully about who uses our services, how they use them, and how we support them. We determined early on that we were going to be a program based not in faith, but in fact.

In 2016, the State of Michigan removed Skyline from its list of focus schools, and while equity gaps still existed and work remained, the data clearly showed that the Writing Center was part of the reason literacy inequities decreased and that our mission to be a third space was a success. As these achievements brought additional attention to our program, the Writing Center has also progressed in slowly shifting teacher and student conversations about writing processes, even outside of English classes, helping students feel more confident about their writing and about themselves as writers beyond traditional grading systems. The Writing Center also has laid the groundwork for other peer-to-peer programs in math and restorative justice at Skyline by showing that students can be trusted to tackle complex issues with thoughtful maturity and radical empathy. What started with a defining moment has become a vast array of student supports and an evolving writing culture.

Beyond Skyline, the success of the Writing Center has allowed us to take a regional approach to confronting literacy inequity by developing meaningful partnerships with other area schools and local university and community writing centers. These collaborations have allowed us to do combined tutor training and development and site-based community work in third spaces off campus, particularly in elementary schools, where equity gaps often have their roots. This work, like our work at Skyline, focuses on relationships first, elevating students' stories over the school stuff. At family fun nights sponsored by a local university, elementary students write stories in their own language or have fun at one of several stations set up with short literacy activities. We participate as both mentors and a willing audience for students' stories. The ability to collaborate with like-missioned partners in this way has allowed us to create system-wide urgency around literacy disproportionality by defining regional literacy needs and advocating for networked solutions based on our shared values.

As a result of working with regional partners, I was accepted into the State of Michigan's Innovative Educator Corps in 2018, which provided financial support for our network to mentor and support local teachers wanting to open writing centers in their schools that could disrupt inequitable practices and build literacy, community, and equity. The initial cohort featured teachers from six schools who received support in learning more about writing centers, building strong program foundations, training and supporting student tutors, supporting school literacy initiatives in a third space, and program assessment and evaluation. Tutors also worked together on prioritizing growth with writers, providing meaningful feedback, and working with reluctant writers.

Moving from a nascent idea about literacy support in a single school to being part of a regional effort for literacy equity has been an intentional and slow process of building a student-centered, student-led program supported by data and rooted in core values that are tied to institutional and local values and that clearly communicate our mission and vision. The process entailed engaging others in strategic ways to change the narrative about the value of writing, the role of writing centers, and the capacity of youth—an advocacy moment collaboratively envisioned and thoughtfully executed by writing center tutors.

What We Noticed as We Read This Chapter

By the end of Jeff Austin's chapter on advocacy within his local community, he has remarkably shifted our perspectives about the possibilities of writing, the spaces where it takes place, and the challenges of preserving such environments. He flips the traditional perspective of what a writing center is from a seemingly dry set of practices to a complete reevaluation of young people's ability to write and read. Jeff and his peer tutors take on the role of advocates for the writing center they continue to develop. Realizing that just building a center is not enough, Jeff shows us how they bring in community and administrative support, developing allies and employing savvy strategies along the way. In this regard, Jeff's chapter also encourages us to reflect on challenging questions: *What does advocacy mean when scratching beneath surface level interpretations of equity? How do we ingrain our practices in ways that can live beyond individual efforts?* Among the themes we noticed:

- *Advocacy often comes from a sense of urgency.* Jeff describes how he came to this work with a sense of urgency that is both personal and "system wide."

  Questions to consider: What are the urgencies you feel surrounding your teaching? How might your gut reactions and interests can help convert inertia to change?

- *Advocacy demands learning.* It is clear that Jeff had plenty to learn as he took on this work. Notice the ways he discovers and researches policy processes around student achievement and writing center scholarship. What we know about the topics we engage in may be limited. While allies may help with this, getting up to speed on the details related to your advocacy topic will take time and energy.

  Question to consider: Where might you turn to learn more about the advocacy issue with which you are engaged?

- *The young people we serve sit at the heart of advocacy work.* As the name Writing Center implies, young people—their academic needs, their leadership capacities, their interests—are the *center* of this work. In light of this, we want to emphasize that advocacy that centers on students often requires adult capital to drive change; our positionality—as adults, as well as based on race, gender, and other assumed identity markers—are forms of capital that we bring with us into the work of advocacy. Jeff highlights his commitment to students through his role as a leader within the school site, and he helps create change through a bevy of skills.

Questions to consider: Who are the young people that are most impacted by the urgent issues you see at the center of your advocacy work? What is the impact of their positionality—and yours—in moving forward with this work?

- *Youth are important allies.* Like Jeff, we believe young people can take ownership over their education. Historically, adults (including teachers and other school officials) have demonstrated skepticism about young people's ability to lead and effect change, but we recognize that youth often lead the charge in activist and civil rights movements. In our own experiences researching with and learning alongside young people, we too often have noticed that students are considered ignorant as to what is in their best interests. Youth advocacy efforts are often met with coddling compliments that do not validate students as holding real power. Instead of placing youth in situations where they could face patronizing comments from adults (e.g., *That's so cute*), Jeff's advocacy efforts focus on how his adult power supports and works in allyship with his youth partners.

  Questions to consider: What role might students play in your advocacy work? How might you develop them as allies, without placing them in unsafe situations?

- *Advocacy and teaching can work hand-in-hand.* As Jeff writes in the chapter, "Over the next two years, we developed a social justice and equity statement that forced us to examine our implicit biases and the systemic inequities around us and to develop a plan to work against both." Those are lofty demands on the kind of space that he is working to sustain. Recognizing that youth power resides in the relationships fostered alongside conversations of equity, Jeff hints at a theory of change that suggests that engagement in advocacy efforts—from students and teachers alike—can yield rewarding results in ELA classrooms; effective teaching can occur in tandem with purposeful advocacy efforts.

  Question to consider: What shifts (curricular or pedagogical) might you make in your own teaching to support a stance on advocacy alongside your students?

Looking at Jeff's description of his efforts and his journey, we are reminded that advocacy efforts focused on a single school site can have rippling effects. Considering the ways Jeff developed savvy skills for expanding stakeholder interest and building legitimacy for the writing center, we encourage you to consider how this might look in your own community. Consider how your teaching contexts could parallel Jeff's emphasis on designs that center on student needs.

Chapter 5

Post, Share, Tag, Comment, Tweet

Harnessing Social Media for Professional Development and Advocacy

Kristen R. Strom

Kristen Strom returned to the classroom as a secondary ELA teacher after her recent completion of a PhD at Illinois State University. In this chapter she challenges us to consider how social media can be used to support advocacy efforts and to help others (colleagues, administrators, beginning teachers, parents, and community members) learn more about teaching practices and their connections to research.

While scrolling through my professional Facebook account, I find my post about Literature Circles and tag Meghan in the comments so she can browse the linked resources for an upcoming unit she's planning. Meghan recently joined my classroom as my student teacher, and we connect electronically after school hours to share ideas for upcoming lessons. A few days later while checking my Twitter feed, I read educators' responses to a question about the ways they incorporate music and poetry into their classrooms; I take a screenshot and send Meghan the image of the teacher's comment about comparing/contrasting Kendrick Lamar's "Pray for Me" with Claude McKay's "If We Must Die" (a poem from our Harlem Renaissance Unit). And during the first week of February, her cell phone buzzes with a screenshot from Instagram that is meant to motivate us to create our own classroom display of literary works by African American authors to celebrate African American history month (Figure 5.1).

These examples demonstrate some of the ways social media influences my classroom activities and my collaborations with colleagues, parents, and education scholars across the nation. They also speak to the ways in which advocacy—in our digital age—is intertwined with social media and can be used to change the narrative about literacy education. Twenty-first-century teaching calls for educators to use their media/digital presence in their conversations with colleagues, administrators, parents, community members; those interactions—when done wisely—can help change the narrative surrounding education education by highlighting innovative teaching strategies and student learning. In addition, literacy educators can model for their students how a thoughtful digital presence can lead to change and encourage students to consider how they can advocate for change while using social media platforms.

Reviewing the Facebook, Instagram, and Twitter pages that I follow provides a plethora of opportunities to improve my pedagogy: I read articles about teaching diverse student populations, I gather resources for units of study, and I find inspiration to modify my instruction, planning, and assessment practices. Social media provides free networking and professional development. By scrolling my sites, I can learn *from* and *with* educators, parents, and other individuals involved in educating our youth. The educators and professional organizations I follow become my allies in this work, and they inspire me to improve my own practice, to carry out school-wide initiatives, and to advocate for my students and the teaching profession. (The National Council of Teachers of English [NCTE], for example, encouraged me to collaborate with my

Figure 5.1 Instagram Post on Classroom Display

colleagues to plan and carry out a Banned Book Week celebration and an African American Read-In.)

My own social media posts advocate for the use of various best practices of literacy instruction, of culturally responsive and sustaining teaching practices, and of making visible the teaching, learning, leading, and mentoring that take place in today's modern classrooms. My goal is to create and/or share content 2 to 3 days per week on my professional sites. I attempt to balance my posts with an array of resources. Before I opened my social media sites, I carefully considered my purpose. Questions I continue to ask myself include

- Why did I create this professional page?
- Who is my audience?
- What types of posts/information/resources communicate my purpose and are relevant to my audience?
- What message(s) do I want to communicate?
- How can I use this platform's functions and features and my posts to engage my audience, as well as network with and learn from others?
- How can I advocate for the teaching profession and the awesome things teachers and students do every day in our nation's schools?
- How do I consider my students' privacy in terms of posting their pictures and their classwork? (My school district, for example, asks students' parents/guardians to give their permission for their student's picture to be taken and used by the school.)

Regardless of those responses, I always ask my students for permission to take pictures of them and their schoolwork. When I post images of students' work, I make sure their names are not visible.

My professional social media presence began when a professor-mentor from my PhD program encouraged me to start a digital footprint for my teaching and scholarly interests. Because I was most familiar with Facebook, I started there. While I taught an English education methods course to preservice teachers, I used my professional Facebook page to document the literacy teaching methods we studied along with links to educational resources. I shared my page with past and present colleagues, family members, and friends who I thought would be interested in learning about teaching practices, topics in education, and how to meet the needs of diverse learners. I also invited the teacher candidates in my courses to follow my page, to use it as a resource, to remember teaching and assessment methods we learned in the course, and to stay in touch with me during their student teaching placement and also after graduation.

When I returned to the secondary English language arts (ELA) classroom, after completing my PhD program, I continued to use Facebook, but I also opened an Instagram account to highlight the activities I use in my classroom, samples of student work, links to educational articles, NCTE celebrations and initiatives I integrate into my classroom and school, and an abundance of resources on various teaching methods, some of which include Book Talks, Socratic Seminars, and cooperative learning activities. My social media posts demonstrate how I use relevant and engaging literacy teaching and assessment practices, and they include links to resources and articles so that my followers—many of whom are teachers and parents—can both know about and also explore using those literacy practices with their students and children. I also use social media to discuss my scholarly work and research interests, as well as my personal and professional reading and writing habits; in doing so, I promote the importance of being a lifelong learner, reader, and writer. I frequently include images of my professional development activities, such as my participation at professional conferences and my school's "Dunlap U" class periods (see Figure 5.2) where we demonstrate and/or observe effective learning activities that are connected to the Danielson Framework for Teaching.

Social media enables me to mentor the preservice teachers that I continue to teach at various institutions, my student teachers, and educators who follow my pages. I frequently support my previous students by messaging them throughout the year to offer encouragement, ask about their school year, and respond to their social media posts. If individuals comment on my posts, I offer brief replies to their

Figure 5.2   Instagram Post on Professional Conferences

dr_kristenstrom

♡ ◯ ▽   ⊓

Liked by **heyitsemilybauer** and **26 others**

dr_kristenstrom Dunlap U observation in @snyderanne classroom. Students are in learning centers rotating around the room learning about JFKs presidency. Small groups of students are in charge of the daily topic: today is Cuba, yesterday was Civil Rights, and tomorrow is Cold War/ Vietnam. Such a creative way to allow students agency over their learning!
My mind is spinning with how to adapt this project for my ELA classroom. Any ideas?!

comments and/or questions, and if needed, I use the platform's messaging feature to provide more detailed information. I also reach out to other educators for resources, advice, and professional opportunities by commenting on their posts or sending them a personal message. Browsing my social media feeds offers abundant opportunities to learn, network, and share resources with others; however, I am cognizant of spending too much time with it. I limit my use of social media to certain times during the day when my schedule allows and after school when I am researching ideas for upcoming units of study.

Now that the preservice teachers I instructed are teaching in their own ELA classrooms, many of them use their social media sites to showcase their classroom instruction and activities. With their permission, I share their posts on my Facebook page to spotlight their innovative teaching methods and students' products (see Figure 5.3), as well as their personal reflections on teaching. Sometimes they reach out to me for additional resources or feedback, and other times I ask them to share their teaching ideas so I can replicate them with my own students. Collectively, we are everyday advocates for the enriching experiences we are providing our students in diverse classroom and school settings.

Figure 5.3 Facebook Post on Classroom Innovations

Kristen R. Strom
March 12 · 🌐

Proud teacher moment-

One of my ISU preservice teachers is now teaching full time in his own ELA classroom. Check out the beautiful work his students produced for an assignment where they were asked to depict the major conflict of the story (The House on Mango Street) in the first two boxes, depict Cisneros' use of imagery in the next, theme in the next, and the protagonist in the final. Then, they had to fill out the border with quotes/art/and words from the text that represent the overall feeling of the text.

It's this "stuff"- of adolescents and classrooms and teacher creativity- that warms my soul. When teachers give students opportunities to show their talents beyond traditional assignments, our students get the chance to shine.

Bravo, Mr. H! I am so very proud.

When I met Meghan, weeks before the start of her student teaching placement, I shared my professional Facebook page with her so that she could browse my posts from the previous semester. I hoped that by browsing the resources, images, and articles on my page, she could get a sense of my teaching philosophy and the culture of my secondary ELA classroom. After the first week of Meghan's student teaching placement and the number of screenshots I shared with her through text message, I realized how important it was for her to become active on social media for her own professional development and networking. I encouraged her to create professional Facebook, Instagram, and/or Twitter accounts that would remain separate from her personal accounts. She decided to use Instagram to highlight the creative activities and assessments she plans, creates, and carries out. As a new teacher beginning to network with other professionals, the hashtag function on Instagram provides a larger network of followers and people to follow. Less than 24 hours after starting her Instagram journey, she arrived to school excited to show me her new account, resources she wanted to incorporate into future units of study, her followers and the people and hashtags she follows, and how she planned to use her page to showcase the innovative work taking place in our classroom. During interviews for her first teaching job, Meghan discussed her use of Instagram for professional development to show administrators how she uses best practices in her classroom and how she learns from other educators through the digital platform. Once she accepted a job, she followed the social media sites of her future colleagues and school so that she could begin to learn about the school's culture, students, and programs. Now that Meghan has her own ELA classroom, she continues to use Instagram to showcase her teaching and students' learning. She reports that after modeling her use of social media to her new colleagues, a handful of them have started to use social media for professional development and to demonstrate their teaching methods and student work.

Another form of social media that is connected to my advocacy work is blogging. After reflecting on the lack of professional development available to some teachers within their school districts and how social media has helped improve my ELA pedagogy, I realized that I, personally, can support educators and mentor new teachers through a professional blog. In the era of public-school budget cuts, K–12 teacher professional development and mentoring programs are often unfunded. Research shows that the most successful new teachers are those supported by effective mentors (Gray & Taie, 2015). Discussions with my student teacher and other colleagues who were beginning their teaching careers led me to launch a blog to connect with new teachers entering the profession with teacher mentors. My blog provides resources, mentorship, and encouragement for carrying out effective teaching practices and advocating for change in teachers' classrooms and schools. While my blog is still in the beginning stages, it is another way to connect with teachers from a range of teaching experiences and to make apparent the resilience of teachers who continue to advocate for themselves, their students, their schools, and the profession.

My social media feeds, as well as those I view of other educators across the country, and my blog provide a counter narrative to the negative reports on educational issues in mainstream media. When educators make visible the positive experiences in classrooms and harness social media for professional development, networking, and mentoring, we become everyday advocates for effective literacy, teaching, and learning practices that influence students and teachers beyond our own school settings.

What We Noticed as We Read This Chapter

According to data from the Pew Research Center (Perrin & Anderson, 2019), nearly 70% of all adults in the United States are Facebook users. Other than You-Tube, Facebook is the most commonly used social media platform in use as we write this. And while recent political discussions have raised important questions about the responsibilities of social media companies and the kinds of information shared and sold across these sites, we are cautiously excited about the possibility of social media as an avenue for everyday advocacy, as Kristen Strom explores in this chapter.

Though Kristen shares numerous approaches to connecting social media and advocacy in her chapter, we want to highlight a couple that are immediately actionable by readers.

- *Leveraging social media to show schooling in real life.* Through her Instagram account, Kristen uses social media to provide a unique peek into real classrooms today. Though we recognize that pictures may need to be modified to protect student identities, this can be done, and then the images can be used to inform a broader public about school life today. Such posts may—as Kristen highlights—include lesson plans, reflections on instruction, and samples of student work (if your students, parents, and school local policies are okay with it).

Questions to consider: How might you use social media to show the teaching and learning happening in your classroom? What platforms (Instagram, Facebook, Twitter, YouTube channels) might work for you and the audiences you want to reach?

- *Using social media to develop allies.* Kristen demonstrates the ways these networks bring together the fundamental "social" aspects of social media. Closed and private Facebook groups have been useful in our professional lives to connect us to broader communities of English educators across the country, including organizations like the National Council of Teachers of English and the National Writing Project; without sustained engagement with friends in online groups, we would not feel as connected to these larger organizations. Kristen's use of social media brings together peers who are distributed across time zones to focus on particular issues and to bring insights to the localized issues we may be working on.

  Questions to consider: What networks are you already a part of? What networks might you join? How can these networks (professional ones with other English educators or more local ones in your own school district) be used to develop allies?

- *Using social media as "smart" advocacy.* We want to point out that the streams of dialogue and learning that are possible in online spaces are "smart" forms of advocacy—taking in perspectives from varied sources and stakeholders helps strengthen the work that we do in classrooms today. Amid current fears of breaches of privacy, of the circulation of false information, and of online bullying, we forget the simple fact that social networks are *social*. Kristen highlights a dizzying number of practices she engages in to build on the crowdsourcing of digital social networks. Her classroom is immediately connected to an unseen, vast array of participants who share ideas and can help her improve her practice. As you engage in advocacy efforts for and with your students, consider whose voices, perspectives, and expertise might help shape the work you do—and also whose voices should not.

Question to consider: How might you, as a smart advocate, make sure you are connecting to legitimate sources and forwarding accurate information? (We remember a recent report that circulated on social media claiming that researchers had "solved" the reading wars, claiming a phonics-only approach was scientifically proven. We are saddened by the magnitude of people this reached and who might be swayed by what we consider a not-so-scientific report.)

- *Using your online presence in safe ways.* As you decide how you might use social media to boost your own advocacy efforts, consider some specific approaches. Kristen distinguishes her online presence in this chapter as a "professional social media presence" that is separate from personal posts, which might focus on family, hobbies, or interpersonal relationships unrelated to work. In contrast, Antero's Twitter feed is a veritable smorgasbord of content—from research-focused discussions to participation in education chats like the #NCTEchat to geeky affinities for pop culture and bad puns. There is no separation between what Antero posts for "work" and what he posts for a less academically-oriented audience. These are choices each of us must make about how we present ourselves to a broader, digital public.

Questions to consider: What might be considered "safe" ways to post in your own context? What ways of posting make sense for the particular issues you engage in?

References

Gray, L., & Taie, S. (2015). *Public school teacher attrition and mobility in the first five years: Results from the first through fifth waves of the 2007–08 beginning teacher longitudinal study* (NCES 2015–337). U.S. Department of Education. Washington, DC: National Center for Education Statistics.

Perrin, A. & Anderson, M. (2019). Share of U.S. adults using social media, including Facebook, is mostly unchanged since 2018. *Pew Research Center.* Retrieved from https://www.pewresearch.org/fact-tank/2019/04/10/share-of-u-s-adults-using-social-media-including-facebook-is-mostly-unchanged-since-2018/

Chapter 6

Composing Advocacy as Teacher–Writers

Christine Dawson, Christina Ponzio, Nora Liu Robinson, Jillian VanRiper, Kelly Hanson

In their description of supporting advocacy through writing, the five authors of this chapter build on a foundation of solidarity. Centering their own advocacy efforts in their literacy practices, writing group members support each other in planning, composing, enacting, and growing from advocacy efforts across multiple school settings. Even though these teachers write in places that are geographically spread out, the practices that they have nurtured over more than a decade help illustrate the ways advocacy work can thrive within a close-knit community.

It's 7:00 Eastern time on a Tuesday night, and one by one we each find a quiet space in our homes to log onto our computers and join our Google Hangout. Writing group time! We are situated across three states (and sometimes even multiple countries), but for the past 10 years we've been coming together, at least monthly, to share and grow our writing projects. Jillian now teaches high school English, Nora teaches high school English as an Additional Language, and Kelly teaches middle school French. Christine teaches in a college teacher education program, and Christina is currently pursuing her doctorate in teacher education. While we certainly share our poetry, narratives, and other personal texts, we also have come to see our writing group as a space to develop our voices as advocates, especially as we seek to make change for ourselves, our students, and our programs. During writing group meetings, we articulate ways to move from frustration to action: we decipher first steps, rehearse language, and plan interventions. By considering our advocacy efforts as *acts of composing*, we also help each other build on our writing strengths, knowledge, and strategies.

Our Writing Group

Our writing group formed in 2008, when Nora, Jillian, Christina, and Kelly began their teaching careers. We met during a series of university English methods courses taught by Christine, and we formed our group to help us pursue our own writing projects. We also sought a means to support each other as we scattered across the state and country into various new roles as educators. We meet online, using Skype or Google Hangout to host video meetings, so that we can talk about our writing in real time. We made this choice early on because we valued the opportunity to both build our relationships with each other and talk through writing projects at all stages. We also use a private, online space to share our writing (we've moved from a wiki to Google Docs over the years). (See the box for suggestions for starting a writing group.)

We always begin our meetings with an opportunity to reconnect with each other, to discuss our lives and happenings. Each person then has an opportunity to share their writing, whether the text is just an idea or a fully formed draft. The author offers context, as well as goals and special requests for focus, and then the author directs us to read the text she is sharing (usually via Google Docs). We all read the author's text and then discuss, focusing on the author's purpose, asking questions to draw out ideas, explore purpose and audience, and extend the use of strategies. In our writing group discussions we have created a space for a range of writing experiences and opportunities to grow our advocacy work (Dawson, 2017; Dawson, Robinson, Hanson, VanRiper, & Ponzio, 2013).

Validation and Support

One of the most significant ways we use our writing group is to help us orally sort through challenges we are experiencing, often before we begin actually writing. Advocacy can feel isolating, especially when we feel like we are raising lone voices for change. It can be easy to question ourselves in these moments: *Why am I the only one who sees a problem?* When we bring an advocacy issue to our writing group, we try to share, with honest detail, the context, issues, and stakeholders who are involved. These descriptions often feel messy at first, and the group helps the speaker clarify their problem, goals, and possible action plan(s).

These initial discussions also help us share the emotional labor of advocacy. By collectively discussing a problem, the group can help absorb the speaker's emotional load—including the frustrations and even disappointment we may experience when we encounter injustice and inequities. Hearing our concerns and values echoed back by other trusted voices can provide valuable support to help move from emotion to action.

Approaching Advocacy as *Writing* Challenges

As a writing group, we frame advocacy efforts as rhetorical challenges, which we can address through familiar writing practices. Just as we often ask about a writer's audience

Suggestions for Starting a Writing Group

- Decide on a place to meet that is convenient for all group members, whether a local cafe or an online platform (e.g., Skype, Zoom, or Google Hangouts).
- Discuss each person's goals for participating in the group, and allow these to shape your decisions about meeting frequency and routines. Be realistic and flexible as members' time commitments shift.
- Build in time for the group to reconnect at the beginning of the meeting; this opportunity to catch up on each other's lives is necessary to foster trust and grow relationships.
- Invite each writer to share writing at any stage of the writing process, whether it's just the seed of an idea or a full draft.
- Ask the writer to specify how the piece was developed, the intentions for the piece, and what kind of feedback would be most valuable.
- When providing feedback, be sure to highlight what is effective about the piece. Follow up with responsive, respectful questions and suggestions to support the writer.
- Invite the writer to share a plan for revision before moving on to the next member.

and purpose when crafting a poem or narrative, we reach for these familiar questions when a member engages in advocacy: *What do you want to accomplish? Where is your energy in this project? Who is your audience and what do they care about?* These clarifying conversations help frame next steps, especially as we orally unpack our priorities. While a group member may, ultimately, want to change a policy or create an opportunity, we also acknowledge other goals, such as being heard and building (or preserving) relationships with multiple stakeholders such as administrators and colleagues.

As teacher–writers, we often consider how written texts may be useful in our advocacy work. Sometimes writing a simple email to request a meeting can frame a later conversation in useful ways. Sometimes a bulleted proposal will help visually connect our ideas with an audience's interests. And sometimes the most significant writing we do is for ourselves, as we craft an outline or flowchart to help us plan our own actions. In any case, we can share our written texts during our meetings to help focus our writing group conversations on the purpose, audience, effect, arrangement, genre, and style of our writing and advocacy efforts.

Clarifying and Redefining Purpose to Enlist Allies: Nora's Advocacy

As we collaboratively examine a problem of practice, our conversations often help us clarify or revise our purpose. For example, Nora had been working for several years to help her English learners feel more successful in their academic and art courses. In her efforts to help bridge these gaps, she had been creating a website for English learners, featuring common vocabulary, expressions, and grammatical structures of various disciplines (e.g., history, math, music, visual arts). She was trying to expand the use and reach of her site, so she contacted other content teachers to gather examples of discipline-specific language that she could add. But despite multiple overtures, she was not getting responses from the content teachers, and her website felt anemic.

When Nora shared this challenge with our group, talking through her frustrations and the inertia she was experiencing, she began to redefine her problem and purpose. She realized she had been taking on the primary responsibility for teaching her students how to access academic language, inadvertently positioning her colleagues as external obstacles to these efforts. She felt like she was hitting a wall. Through our conversations, she was able to reframe the way she considered her colleagues; rather than viewing them as an outside audience to persuade, she began to position them as collaborative partners in a joint effort. This shift allowed Nora to redirect and renew her energy, ultimately shaping a roundtable discussion she facilitated at the TESOL International Association's Annual Convention.

Defining Purpose and Framing an Issue: Christina's Advocacy

As we help each other clarify purpose and audience, we often "rehearse" language and plan texts to help us enter advocacy conversations. For example, early in her teaching career Christina was the de facto English as a Second Language district coordinator, and she needed to present her administrators with updates to federal Title III and Office of Civil Rights guidance. During one writing group meeting, Christina shared three-and-a-half pages of legislative jargon, explanations of Title III requirements, and first-draft thinking about implications for her district. She knew she needed a concise presentation and a strategy to diplomatically present this information to her administrators. But she was stuck.

Talking through her context and goals helped Christina define her purposes for her upcoming presentation: to provide critical updates, to clarify budgeting restrictions (which had implications for her own salary), and to advocate for the program priorities she was setting. Our group discussion helped Christina separate her own goals from those of her administrators, and she began to strategically plan two texts to help her focus and frame this information for her audience. She decided to create a PowerPoint presentation with the legal updates and a written handout that highlighted her own programmatic goals and advocacy. Christina also used our writing group to orally rehearse for her meeting, refining her word choice based on her audience and purposes. By the end of our writing group discussion, she had a clear outline for her PowerPoint and handout, as well as oral practice explaining her key points.

Reaching Multiple Audiences: Jillian's Advocacy

While some of our advocacy projects have a primary target audience, in others we must reach multiple stakeholders, each of whom has a different interest. As her school's writing department chair, Jillian noticed that she and her colleagues were struggling to implement writing workshop pedagogies in their classrooms. Though the school had brought in experts to facilitate several professional development workshops, Jillian was finding this model frustrating and ineffective. Based on her work in our writing group and with the National Writing Project, Jillian wanted to create a year-long opportunity for writing teachers to set their own learning goals, engage in collective inquiry, and participate in peer coaching. She knew this approach was different from the standard professional development model her district was using, and she also knew it would be an unfamiliar model for most of her colleagues. Therefore, Jillian needed to reach out to her colleagues, as well as school and district-level administrators, in her advocacy efforts.

Our writing group helped Jillian think through the various interests of these different audiences and consider specific written texts to best engage each stakeholder. For her principal and superintendent, Jillian realized she would need a formal proposal that explained why her program met the school and district professional development goals and how it could be implemented. The superintendent would also need to see that funding the proposal would fit within budgetary boundaries. For her colleagues, Jillian planned an email with an overview of the program and an invitation to attend an informational meeting. She also planned an agenda for that first meeting, during which she would elaborate on her ideas and lead the group in making preliminary organizational decisions.

Talking through these audiences and texts helped Jillian flesh out her ideas and anticipate potential obstacles. She realized that she was most worried about recruiting enough colleagues and ensuring that they would find the experience beneficial rather than obligatory. She drew on her past experiences as a writing group member to help connect with her peers and emphasize the goals and benefits of this professional development endeavor. The hopes she articulated were rooted in the experiences that keep her coming back to our writing group: that this professional development process can directly serve each member of the group by providing support, validation, and targeted learning to address individual teaching concerns. In the end, Jillian was successful in starting the program, and her colleagues noted substantial growth in their teaching practices, investment in the writing workshop model, and sense of leadership and community in the school building.

Conclusion

Over the past ten years, the five of us have helped each other raise our voices for students and colleagues, for instructional opportunities and educational supports. Across

Suggestions for Using a Writing Group to Promote Advocacy

- Consider advocacy as acts of composing, so you can draw upon your writing knowledge and experiences to support your efforts.
- Collectively nurture your identity, values, and authority as a writer and change-maker.
- Draw from your group's strength to stay grounded and build resilience.
- Discuss when and how to enter a conversation.
  - Analyze the context and audience of your advocacy. (What are their values? Interests?)
  - Clarify or redefine the purpose and desired effect of your advocacy.
  - Consider how you can use text(s) to help frame or mediate your efforts. What content, genre, organization, style, tone, and mode will help you best meet your purpose with this audience?
  - Rehearse your interactions and responses (orally and in writing).
- View change and overcoming challenges as an ongoing process of composing and revision.

these experiences, we have found that positioning advocacy in terms of *composing* has helped us draw on our writing knowledge and strategies so that we are more confident speaking out. As you engage in your own advocacy efforts, we recommend finding a trusted friend or colleague who can help you approach advocacy the same way you might compose a text. Through talk and writing, help each other clarify the context of your situation, the problem you are seeking to address, your purpose for entering the conversation, the stakeholders who are involved, and the outcome(s) you hope to achieve. Support each other through the emotional labor of this work, validating each other's intentions and clarifying (and even revising) your visions for action and change. Craft entrance points and mediating texts that fit your context and goals. And share your experiences across these stages with your thinking partners, so that you may notice and build on strategies to raise your voices in our profession.

What We Noticed as We Read This Chapter

In our experience as writers, researchers, and former teachers, we have encountered friends and colleagues who name their feelings of isolation—in schools and universities away from their familiar communities—as a substantial reason for why their writing halts and their advocacy efforts do not move forward. In this chapter, the four authors demonstrate a far different scenario: a long-term, collaborative writing group that support each member's advocacy moves. We want to highlight what we noticed about how that collaboration works.

- *Collaboration can be advanced by simple or more advanced technologies.* The simple and the fancy tools and technologies available to us today facilitate our engagement in advocacy and learning with a writing group; our phones and our computers make it possible to traverse the boundaries of time and space to forge new ways of learning with our colleagues

  Questions to consider: What technologies do already use that might facilitate collaboration? What others have you heard of (or read about in this chapter) that you would like to learn? How might those foster collaboration?

- *Collaboration requires a deep commitment.* Showing up to recurring meetings—because it matters to students and to our professional growth—takes discipline, commitment, and patience. Friendship, of course, drives this as well, but we particularly appreciate seeing the deep commitment to the work of advocacy that this chapter elucidates. The emotional labor required in engaging in advocacy (as well as nearly every dimension of teaching) is quite clear in the voices of this chapter. Relationships must always be at the heart of the work we do, and these five educators help us see that. Discussing, imagining collectively, offering feedback, revising, and generally being vulnerable . . . the work of this group would not be possible without the foundation of trust that develops over time.

Questions to consider: Do you already participate in a writing group like this? If so, how might you facilitate shifting the focus toward advocacy? If not, how might you get one started?

- *Advocates attend to rhetorical considerations.* The authors emphasize the importance of attending to purpose, audience, and genres of writing when writing for advocacy: from emails to proposals to outlines to flowcharts. These rhetorical questions inform what and how they write—whether it's just for themselves or for an external audience.

  Questions to consider: When considering your own advocacy, are their particular audiences who seem most important to reach? What genres might speak well to them? What do you need to consider in terms of tone, language, and organization?

- *Empathetic listening leads to advocacy.* While this chapter is centered on a group of passionate *writers*, we noticed how their time is spent: listening, hearing, and acknowledging the experiences and perspectives of the members. The words are a catalyst for action, for empathy, and for growth.

  Questions to consider: How does time spent in making and sustaining connections among the members of a writers' group translate into empathic advocacy? What might you do to help create and sustain that empathy?

- *Equity matters.* Even as writing and the relational processes that accompany it illustrate the actions of advocacy, equity, another key aspect of advocacy, is also demonstrated in this chapter. In nearly every effort we will engage in as advocates, functional writing provides the key aspects of how we will inch the needle ever closer to equity in the world of education.

  Question to consider: What connections do you see between advocacy and equity?

We encourage readers to take particular note (as we did) of the key suggestions that close this chapter. These teachers, walking readers through several case studies of how their writing group has helped them grow, provide clear suggestions for adapting these practices for your own context. As you consider your local peers and those across broader geographical contexts, consider the double-allyship that your role may embody: these five authors find ways to work in solidarity with one another as well as in synergistic ways with the communities in their own local settings. You have these capabilities, too.

References

Dawson, C. (2017). *The teacher-writer: Creating writing groups for personal and professional growth.* New York: Teachers College Press.

Dawson, C., Robinson, E., Hanson, K., VanRiper, J., & Ponzio, C. (2013). Creating a breathing space: An online teachers' writing group. *English Journal, 102*(3), 93–99.

Chapter 7

Beginning With the Local

Connecting Personal Growth With Advocacy

Rick Joseph

*Rick Joseph, Michigan 2015–2016 Teacher of the Year, teaches fifth and sixth grad-
ers in Birmingham, Michigan. In this provocative chapter, he asks us to consider the
fundamental assumptions of how we see, interpret, and make assumptions of the world
around us. Rooted in Rick's reflection of his personal growth and the biases he carried
into his classrooms in the past, this chapter highlights how our own perspectives must
adapt and shift as we come to see anew the full humanity of the young people in our
classrooms and their literacy needs.*

My name is Rick, and I am a recovering homophobe. I grew up in the
1970s and 1980s in a traditional family environment. I was the product
of a society in which people who were LGBTQ+ were far more likely to
be closeted than out. Everything I knew about them came from mainstream media
stereotypes and incessant pejorative references.

My fears of LGBTQ+ people began to abate soon after high school when I actually
met and worked with people who were LGBTQ+. I listened to their stories. I realized
that they had the same needs, hopes, and dreams that I did. I realized they were people,
just like me.

This budding realization drove me to a new purpose. As an educator, I now seek to help foster a school community where homophobia no longer exists, and safe and inclusive spaces are the norm for every student.

I was drawn to education in the early 1990s to address the opportunity gap that exists between students of color and their white peers. As a bilingual/ELL educator for the first seven years of my career, I faced the reality of structural inequities in the daily lives of the students I served. As a teacher in a predominantly white middle-class suburb, I am similarly aware of persistent social inequities that affect people who are LGBTQ+.

The research surrounding this issue is incontrovertible. According to the 2017 National School Climate Survey (GLSEN, 2018), which has been conducted every other year since 2001, school can be a hostile and unsafe place for students who are LGBTQ+. While learning environments have become more inclusive overall, there are still significant numbers of students who are harassed and bullied because of their real or perceived sexual orientation and/or identity. The suicide rate for transgender adolescents is up to four times that of cisgender peers. The homeless population across the country contains a disproportionately high number of LGBTQ+-identified people.

My commitment to supporting LGBTQ+ students and creating change in how schools shift the conversation led me to an advocacy stance. I would encourage colleagues who are similarly interested in changing schools, changing classrooms, and changing public stances toward youth to think about how everyday advocacy could help. As I did, you might begin from a point of inquiry—*What's that issue that concerns you so deeply?*—and then by thinking about that issue in terms of your local context: *What are the greatest needs in the communities in which you work? How can you best raise awareness and heighten consciousness through an examination of the stories of the people that represent these communities?*

I have found that this local, grassroots sensibility turns classroom teachers into sometimes reluctant advocates. Some people are pulled into daily advocacy after experiencing some kind of personal trauma; others simply identify a local need and realize ways to fill it.

My deep concern about the LGBTQ+ students I teach has provided me the opportunity to be a part of this work at both the classroom and policy level. In 2016, the year I was named Michigan Teacher of the Year, part of my policy-level advocacy platform was to change the narrative surrounding these students. In that role, my voice was heard differently it is when I spoke as a classroom teacher, and I raised my voice proudly and strategically to work with others to create change. One important step was supporting the establishment of the Michigan State Board of Education's "Statement and Guidance on Safe and Supportive Learning Environments for Lesbian, Gay, Bisexual, Transgender, and Questioning (LGBTQ) Students." (Michigan State Board, 2016). This document provides information and resources to schools so they can best support the most vulnerable students, such as allowing students to use the bathroom that matches their gender identity and referring to kids by their preferred name and pronouns.

At the 2018 NCTE Convention, I was invited to deliver the keynote address for the session entitled *Amplifying and Celebrating Intersectional and Transectional LGBTQ+ Voices.* My remarks emphasized the critical role that the narrative voice plays in raising awareness around the successes and struggles of the LGBTQ+ community. I stressed that we are transformed when we hear a previously unknown story. When a listener or reader is exposed to a new narrative, the character ceases to be "other" and becomes more fully human. This increased level of empathy is critical in establishing safe and inclusive school communities that promote more empathic classroom environments.

The heart of the most effective daily advocacy in a school context, however, involves the students. When students are bridging the gap between classroom theory and real-world practice, their level of engagement is high. Furthermore, engagement cannot be faked. Students bring a level of authenticity to advocacy that is refreshing and motivating. Teachers who listen to and empower their students will realize a profound level of meaning in the work. For me, changing the narrative about LGBTQ+ students begins with how we see our role as teachers: both in the classroom atmosphere we create and in the curricular choices we make. As a 5th and 6th grade teacher, I let my students know that they are welcome, no matter who they are. There is a sign hanging outside my door that declares my classroom to be a safe space for all people. I emphasize this principle by reading the book *I Am Jazz* aloud to my students. The story chronicles the life and transition of Jazz Jennings, a transgender girl. The theme of the story, "be who you are," resonates with my students and establishes an atmosphere that is welcoming and inclusive.

This ethos is embodied in our classroom library, a critically important resource that contains hundreds of titles from multiple genres. Every year, my students and I cocreate the categories for the library. Inspired by Donalynn Miller's work, I want to make sure that students have books at their fingertips, that they actively own their independent reading life, and that I have the ability to continuously supply kids with books that match their needs and interests.

This year, inspired by Caitlin Ryan and Jill Herman-Wilmarth's book *Reading the*

Rainbow, I knew it was time for a category of books in the LGBTQ+ genre. I knew I needed my students to understand and cocreate this genre of our classroom library. I began by asking them to consider groups of people who have been treated unfairly in our country just because of who they are. They created an extensive list of marginalized groups. I then asked them to consider this question, "How would hearing stories about the lives of people from these groups help all people understand them better?" The students quickly established that stories build empathy and that empathy changes people's hearts and minds. One group, however, had not been mentioned in our list: LGBTQ+ people. I asked the students if they had ever heard anyone make fun of somebody because they were or were thought to be LGBTQ+. They all raised their hands.

At that point, I reviewed some age-appropriate definitions of LGBTQ+. I then taught them the term *intersectionality*—a condition that exists when a person belongs to more than one group of people that has been treated unfairly. Next, I borrowed from Oakland University a collection of picture books for children featuring characters who were LGBTQ+.

I asked my students to work together with a partner and do a "book pass," where they examine the book and read as much of it as they can in three minutes. The students were asked to work together to write a response to the question "How could this story help people who experience intersectionality?" for each book. Their responses ranged from, "This book can show people that being gay or lesbian is okay, and that your parents can be of the same gender," (*Heather Has Two Mommies*) to "Dresses are okay to wear for everyone" (*10,000 Dresses*). My 5th and 6th grade students also noted that "More people can understand that people can love whoever they want to love even if it's a boy and boy or girl and girl" (*And Tango Makes Three*) and it's OK to "Speak up, be who you are" (*Morris Mickelwhite and the Tangerine Dress*).

The students' responses and new awareness of ways to address intersectionality validated the presence and utility of the LGBTQ+ book bin in our classroom library. These stories fulfill a potentially lifesaving role in normalizing the experiences of people who are LGBTQ+ in our classroom and in the larger community, beyond our school. Our students, all of them, deserve nothing less.

People have asked me if I sought permission from my administrator before pursuing my intersectionality book pass. The answer is no—because I know my administrator well enough to believe that he would support my use of literature featuring themes and characters from the LGBTQ+ community in a classroom library setting that promotes choice. I feel fully supported and empowered by the atmosphere in my school, which has been cocreated by the administration and classroom teachers. I made the decision to do what I did as a responsible educator.

Thus, another aspect of advocacy that this demonstrates is the need to create allies along the way: from parents to administrators to members of the community. When teachers take the time to know their administrators and the families in the community, as well as the priorities and dispositions that drive them, they can be sensitive to the social and political realities of the communities they serve and proceed strategically.

What We Noticed as We Read This Chapter

We view Rick Joseph's chapter not only as a representation of multiple kinds of organizing and leadership strategies but also as a form of advocacy itself—paying particular attention to supporting our LGBTQ+ students (and, we would add, colleagues and parents).

While Rick's positionality as a teacher of the year has provided him with a broader platform for advocacy than many readers may be afforded, his process remains imperative to how we engage in advocacy. Notice how his work emphasizes these key dimensions of advocacy:

- *Identifying your story of self.* Recalling the words of Marshall Ganz (2011) and his belief in storytelling as advocacy (see Chapter 1), we are drawn to the first paragraphs of this piece. Rick voices the beliefs he once held about people who identify as LBGTQ and how his beliefs shifted when he learned others' stories.

  Questions to consider: What is your story of self, especially in relationship to the advocacy issue that you care about? How has that story shifted over time? What contributed to those shifts?

- *Identifying the local constituents that are fundamental to the advocacy work.* Rick sees students, both locally and globally, at the center of his advocacy and focuses on how he can create a safe and welcoming space for all students, but especially for those who identify as LGBTQ+. His tactics run the gamut, from curricular choices to policy changes.

  Questions to consider: Who is your constituency? Whom will your advocacy most benefit?

- *Analyzing the necessary levers of change within a particular topic and in a particular context.* Rick has had the opportunity to effect change at various levels—within his own classroom, within his school and local community, and at the state and national level. Within each of these settings, he has identified and analyzed the best ways to promote change, from shifting reading choices to creating safe spaces to working strategically with others to establish policy statements at a state level. Each of these occurs in settings that require unique strategic and savvy approaches. And each requires an understanding of how change works in that particular setting.

  Questions to consider: In what context are you working to promote change? What do you need to know about how systems work in that context? How might you find out?

- *Working from a particular positionality to convey information and speak clearly on the issue around which your advocacy revolves.* Rick leverages his identity as a white male teacher to advocate alongside of and for the literacy needs of LGBTQ+ youth. It is imperative that all of us consider, interrogate, and take on this advocate *alongside* stance. To be clear, advocating within an inequitable society that has marginalized voices and identities requires us to bring our full selves to the fights for literacy that our profession demands.

  Questions to consider: Consider your own positionality. How might you use it to advocate alongside others? How might you draw upon the work of fellow advocates to learn how to do this strategically?

- *Studying and comprehending the undergirding policies that shape our work.* In Chapter 2, we refer to this as working in ways that are smart. It's important to recognize what we know and what we don't know. Rick exemplifies the connections between learning and advocacy at so many levels, from expanding his knowledge base of LGBTQ+ books to learning the intricacies of policy work at the state level. And, of course, Rick's honesty about his own lack of knowledge also led him to learn from the stories of others.

  Questions to consider: What about your background might produce blind spots in your awareness? How might you gain knowledge in those areas?

- *Proactively establishing relationships with administrators and families.* Rick states that he did not seek permission from administrators before engaging in intersectional work. On the one hand, his prominence as a leading teacher meant that he could "safely" (as discussed in Chapter 2) engage in this advocacy. But you can imagine the significance of Rick's outreach to administrators and families—before any particular issue arose—that must be in the backstory of this chapter and that created this context in which his decisions are respected. We encourage you to consider what boundaries you are willing to cross when it comes to what is right for the lives in your classrooms each year that hang in the balance. While we recognize the importance of advocating in safe ways (and doing so in ways that are sustainable over time), we also must remember that, on any given day, our power as teachers and our expertise as perpetually learning pedagogues require us to step in front of the ideas, policies, and actions that cause harm.

  Questions to consider: What are you doing right now to establish relationships with administrators, family, and community members that might help you with future advocacy? What strategies might you use to create stronger connections?

We recognize that saying "You were wrong" is hard. Acting to address harm—and to fully embrace the humanity of all students—is even harder. We recognize the moral imperative at the heart of Rick's journey, and we read his chapter as one that advocates across multiple lines.

References

Ganz, M. (2011). Public narrative, collective action, and power. In Odugbemi, S. & Lee, T. (Eds.), *Accountability through public opinion: from inertia to public action* (pp. 273–289). Washington DC: The World.

Kosciw, J. G., Greytak, E. A., Zongrone, A. D., Clark, C. M., & Truong, N. L. (2018). The 2017 National School Climate Survey: The experiences of lesbian, gay, bisexual, transgender, and queer youth in our nation's schools. New York: GLSEN. (https://www.glsen.org/sites/default/files/2019-10/GLSEN-2017-National-School-Climate-Survey-NSCS-Full-Report.pdf)

Michigan Department of Education. "Statement and guidance on safe and supportive learning environments for lesbian, gay, bisexual, transgender, and questioning (LGBTQ) students." https://www.michigan.gov/documents/mde/SBEStatementon LGBTQYouth_534576_7.pdf

Chapter 8

An Open Door

Twitter as an Advocacy Tool for Teachers and Students

Janelle Bence

Janelle Bence's chapter offers a powerful reflection on how, in her more than 20-year teaching career, her teaching and advocacy practices have recently shifted. Through considering the possibilities of openness, she pushes against the current onslaught of high-stakes testing and invites others to learn from and alongside her. Janelle's efforts at tweeting and posting about life in her classroom are about connecting her teaching practices to "part of something larger" than one teacher; she illustrates how our ongoing media efforts can be intentionally framed as forms of advocacy.

Learning Context

I am in my 20th year of teaching. Needless to say, I've seen many educational trends come and go, each attempting to fill a gap, meet a need, engage more learners. One trend that has remained and shows little sign of ever going away, however, is high-stakes testing.

Sadly, this high-stakes (aka high-stress) atmosphere encumbers real learning that could be happening in our classrooms. This tunnel vision, focused on local, state, and national standardized tests, was meant to ensure a consistent baseline, yet the emphasis has lowered agency, curiosity, and creativity in both learners and educators. Not only that, what the tests assess does not accurately indicate the authentic learning that is possible and that is realized in public schools. As an experienced teacher, I have come to wonder this: How can we shift the narrative about high-stakes testing so that these real learning experiences can be shared, valued, and, ultimately, advocated for by educators?

Openly sharing not only the successes of our students but also the developing lessons that led to these successes is at the heart of advocacy. It is only through opening our doors that real change can happen. Why? Sharing means we are opening our work up to the scrutiny of others. It means educators understand that what is happening in one classroom makes a difference. Sharing makes a difference not because a particular lesson or curricular approach can be replicated and prescribed in every classroom but because sharing offers a point of reference for remixing. It means educators understand that each learning context and each learner has a story worthy of sharing. Sharing is the spotlighting of individual artifacts of authentic learning to help people think differently about education.

Confession time. It's only been during my last third or so of my career that I've felt testing hasn't invaded and impeded my students' learning. It's only recently that I've had the courage to do what I know is right instead of what will be perceived as sound test prep. Once I gained more confidence in my teaching, I began to cherish any autonomy given to me. I recall keeping my strategies somewhat to myself, not because I didn't want to share, but because I was afraid I would be perceived as not preparing my students for the state test. This seemed to be a surefire way to have admin interfere in your process. Attending to the needs of my learners in a meaningful way and situating learning in relevant contexts were subversive acts. I worried about how public I should go.

But in 2012, I took a leap. I left the only school I had ever taught at, the only district I've ever known, to become what's known as an English I facilitator at a small project-based choice school in an affluent and diverse North Texas suburb. In August 2017, I began coteaching a class with a digital media teacher, Kat Saucier. Part of our New Tech Network model is to have interdisciplinary classes in which learners are situated in learning contexts and they do cohesive, collaborative projects. Out of our collaboration and our exploration of the New Tech Network model, the course Critical Literacies was born, a dream come true. The course combines English and digital media, a match made in heaven. This collaboration mirrors the crucial understanding that the development of reading, writing, speaking, and listening skills is supported by the creation of digital products, which we call "digital makes." These makes are pivotal in calling for change in education.

Opening the Door

Let's begin again. I am in my 20th year of teaching, and I love it. I love it so much that I seek every opportunity to share my practice with anyone who will listen. I no longer teach behind a closed door, keeping what happens in the classroom within the four walls. A shift has occurred.

When I'm not teaching and learning in the classroom, I can be found designing projects, making connections with other teachers for authentic opportunities, speaking at conferences, and blogging about my practice. It's not that I think I have all the answers, but I believe my work and the learning of my students can serve as inspiration for other educators.

My classroom and the work we share raise important questions that drive my practice as well as the practices of many other educators. *Why did or didn't this work? Could I adapt this for my own classroom? What would happen if more teachers shared their practice?* My refreshed approach to my practice keeps me in a constant state of open inquiry.

In my eyes, sharing these questions, experiments, strategies, reflections, and opportunities (some may call them failures) speaks to everything public education is, can be, and should be. Public education is about using transparency, collaboration, and reflection to inform our teaching and our learning.

Our school has dozens of tours of visiting educators, organizations, and community members. We share our practices, we answer questions, and many times, these visits offer some rich opportunities for collaboration. Having an open door not only to other educators but also to parents, school board members, and community members allows my practice and what goes on in my classroom to serve as advocacy for public schools. Having that door open also encourages more ideas and inspiration to flow into and out from my classroom, and my learning design has grown from this exchange of ideas.

When tours aren't on campus, I still attempt to offer a glimpse into my practice. Twitter has become a tool many educators frequently use to publish reflections, makes, and informed opinions.

If Not a Test, Then What?

What does all this have to do with education's obsession with standardized testing? Perhaps the focus on testing is a response to educators who believe in learning that is contextualized and adaptive to student needs. Necessarily, these teachers might teach in different ways from each other (depending on their classrooms and their students), which makes understanding whether all students are receiving instruction of essential content skills difficult for administrators who might not know what various educators are doing on any given day. As an extreme response, some districts and campuses have gone so far as to adopt a curriculum where every day each classroom needs to be on the same concept and lesson. When administrators visit classrooms, they expect to see everyone on the same page.

Taking away the creativity of teachers not only stunts their enthusiasm and creativity but also ignores the diverse needs of our learners. It severely limits the connections educators can make with their students because of the resulting inability to personalize instruction.

What, then, is the answer? What might help educators and learners maintain flexibility yet also be accountable? What systems exist that respect teacher autonomy and at the same time ensure that rigor occurs in the classroom and that standards are addressed? The answer for me was opening the door to my classroom, being transparent about my teaching and my students' learning. Sharing our work to the wider public using Twitter, as well as other digital tools, advocates for a change in how we can begin to observe and understand what goes on in the public classroom. Being transparent through social media sits in contrast to standardized measures but gives others a much fuller view of classroom teaching and learning.

Daily Inspiration

If you are going to incorporate social media in the classroom, establishing a connection to authentic and relevant learning is essential. It seems hypocritical to use a platform like Twitter yet avoid exploring topics and events being discussed in this arena. Because of this, many of my activities and lessons are inspired by events, campaigns, and trending hashtags.

Make no mistake. These topics also fit nicely with the cultural and academic demands of my district and campus. The reading and writing required for creating digital multimodal products and tweeting are challenging and respond to several of our state standards.

Take, for example, World Day of Bullying Prevention. This happens annually on October 7. To observe this day, we ask the class to create 100 different short videos of an activity that may deter bullying. Each video shows them doing an act that may deter bullying, such as including someone instead of marginalizing them or doing something that boosts their own self-confidence. Why this activity? Most, if not all, students experience bullying. This activity allows individuals to work together as collectively they create a hundred solutions to or alternatives to bullying. The students are calling for change and action through their learning. Learners are developing their civic identities. They are thinking critically, contributing to an international initiative, and reaffirming important cultural values of our school.

By first creating and then sharing videos like this, we are using social media to show how this teaching style appeals to a diverse group of learners with a wide array of interests and skills. As an educator, I design opportunities that aim to offer a variety of options for satisfying literacy demands. Learners thrive when they struggle to pick and choose how to succeed in these tasks while understanding the various purposes of each of their deliberate choices of words, genre, media, and social media platform.

Be a Part of Something Larger

There are so many opportunities for educators to create rigorous and meaningful activities for their students. Teachers should actively seek such occasions. When doing meaningful activities, students can quickly understand the purpose of applying and developing the skills within the content.

The National Day on Writing is October 20. Since this fell on a Sunday the year I wanted to use it in my curriculum, I looked for another meaningful way for my learners to observe this important day. I knew about a partnership between the National Writing Project (NWP) and the National Parks Service called *Write Out*. Participants are invited to go outside and notice how surroundings influence mood, what some have termed *place-based* writing. As they observe the changes their environment inspires, participants can create any form of response, along with a written component. My students could take pictures or manipulate images they found or already had. They could discuss a place they've been or one they dream of visiting. From this, they could compose in a variety of genres speaking to the impact of that destination.

One student created a paper crane to suggest the calm she felt at Blue Hen Falls. She then photoshopped the cranes onto an image and wrote a short poem that she publicly shared on Twitter (Figure 8.1):

The quiet rush of the water
calm but formidable
soft but fierce
a force to fear and to adore
Listen to the water
whispering its worthy message

Figure 8.1   Student Tweet

Vibha Radhakrishnan
@VibhaR_nthc

Blue Hen Falls in Ohio is by far my favorite place. Nowhere else can make me feel as peaceful as here, I have only perfect memories. The sound of the water can make even the worst day better. @▓▓▓▓▓▓▓ @janelle #SavedByThePBL #NTHCVoice #WriteOut #WhyIWrite #cisdOurStory

Source: https://twitter.com/VibhaR_nthc/status/1185272893397258240

Learners were thrilled when organizations like the National Council of Teachers of English and the National Writing Project started liking, retweeting, and commenting on their tweets. They understood their work was being viewed by others, and they understood that what they did in school mattered. In fact, the above tweet was sent out in an NWP newsletter as a highlight of the #WriteOut campaign on National Writing Day.

Social media shares voices. For my learners, platforms like Twitter add another layer of publishing and advocacy that extends beyond the traditional limits of classroom audiences. Campaigns like #WriteOut and #WhyIWrite informally connect and curate messages focused on similar goals, thereby amplifying stories to create movements of advocacy. In this instance, educators and learners emphasize literacy, creativity, reflection, and place. In one easily digested digital creation, the public gains a glance into what is valued and practiced in public classrooms. From one tweet, the public can begin to think differently about literacy learning.

Learn, Play, Make, Share, Advocate

Advocacy impacts both teachers and students: we educators use social media to portray what real learning looks like in the classroom, thus advocating for changes in standardized testing and curricula as the only means of assessing student learning; our students use social media to feel or be part of social movements. Most importantly, advocacy work doesn't have to be rigid and disciplined. Moments that allow ideas to take seed and provide time for youth to become rooted in their own beliefs and values are needed, moments that provide the time for reflection and the space to tinker with various versions of what could be. Elements of play, creativity, and dreaming are essential to the advocacy process.

As students begin to take ownership of the issues the speak to them, the issues make them speak, and envisioning utopian alternatives to the status quo helps students see the world in a different way. It situates them in a hopeful space, and although this idealistic world of heroes and acts may never become a reality, progress toward such a place is both inspiring and energizing.

Even as I write this chapter, I feel the buzz of excitement in the possibility that my students' work might spark the interest of other educators and motivate them to try something new. I recognize, as well, that these moments of student learning might spark educators, administrators, parents, and board members to broaden their view of what successful literacy education looks like.

Here are some guidelines that shape my design:

1. *Respond to what is happening and current in pop culture, news, or observed days around the world.* This contextualizes you as not only an educator but also as active civic being. It demonstrates flexibility in your practice and highlights the importance of pivoting and being responsive to what unfolds around us.

2. *Allow students to make a product, either digitally or no-tech, that synthesizes their understanding from research.* When learners are able to create, it brings a deeper insight to their knowledge of the content. Learners make deliberate choices on how to represent their understanding, and when these choices are explained and defended, it is clear the process has contributed to the interpretation of information.

3. *Have examples of such products available for students.* Sometimes, learners don't know what's possible. Invite learners to remix ideas to create new possibilities.

4. *Celebrate creativity, play, and imagination.* There's no need for explanation here, but education is lacking this process of tinkering with digital tools to articulate student thinking. Education is worse because of it. Instead, creating while taking risks with digital tools is the beginning of what could be or, at the very least, the beginning of discussions on where we want youth civic life to take us. Learning that encourages the rethinking of the status quo through digital creation challenges learners to cross boundaries, think on a larger scale, and ponder innovative solutions to pressing concerns.

5. *Share these visions through publishing so that this work is seen by more than one teacher.* When people know their work will be seen by others, it gives them that extra push to produce something accurate, creative, and high quality. Use mentions—including Twitter handles to alert potentially interested people of the post—purposefully. Consider potential partners in similar work or who might be interested in seeing the makes. It helps learners see the relevance of their work. Last year, one of the Afrofuturism tweets was liked by Nadji Jeter, the Black dancer, actor, and voice of Miles Morales in Spider-Man television series, chosen by one of my learners who transformed the actor into a superhero because of his many contributions. Knowing their work may be seen by people they respect makes a huge difference.

6. *Keep a consistent hashtag.* Start by discussing all of the digital citizenship practices for your learners. Create "clean" school Twitter accounts to ensure that potential viewers will feel comfortable distributing whatever content is posted. Using a whole-class hashtag like #NTHCVoice has several benefits. First, it allows teachers to find tweets from students without looking at many individual accounts. Second, it acts as a living curation of the work. Third, at any given time, stakeholders and the wider public can view this hashtag for exemplars of thinking and innovative digital creating that is happening in real time in public schools.

Educational Renaissance?

Some may say that being in my 20th year of teaching, I am entering the twilight phase of my career. Yet, in spite of continued mandates of standardized testing as a measure of academic success, I am still here, more energized than ever.

I am determined that stories of real learning will prevail. When learners feel their learning matters and their work is impactful, that is the true sign of transformational education. There are invitations to write, read, create, and share everywhere. We must leverage those to redefine what public education in the United States is and can be.

It is a process. There are many ways to refocus how we evaluate "effective" schools. There will be mistakes along the way, but one thing is for sure: the current state—of standardized tests determining the fates not only of public schools but also of our students—needs to change.

Purposeful design, coupled with social media platforms, allows learners to interact with the world. Students reflect on how events, places, and ideas impact them, and they are given an outlet for sharing their stories, thereby impacting the world around them. Teaching and learning are civic acts that transcend what can be measured by any standardized assessment. It's time to fully realize and honor this.

This change cannot and will not happen overnight, but each step we take makes a difference. Each collaboration, each project, each activity can encourage someone to think differently about education. Each share, each like, each view of a post on social media can make a difference in bracing ourselves for the necessary shift. Perhaps, it will happen one tweet at a time.

What We Noticed as We Read This Chapter

This is a playful chapter that juxtaposes the joy of teaching and the thrill of getting to learn in the company of a broader, international audience. Janelle Bence brings together her interest in learning, her decades-long passion for teaching, and her growing online audience to continually center on advocacy. It is significant that she does so while acknowledging that this work is happening under the high-stakes regime of assessment and accountability. Janelle explores ways of making her practices understandable for a broader audience, and we want to highlight several key themes for you to consider in your practice:

- *Sharing openly is a form of outreach.* There are two important truths we want to point out as we ruminate on Janelle's chapter. On the one hand, offering glimpses into our classrooms can create a world of vulnerability: it is scary to engage in openness. At the same time, sharing not only benefits others—as a form of advocacy—but also invites opportunities for continual growth, feedback, and support.

  Questions to consider: What would it take for you to open up your classroom practices to others? If not all of your teaching practices, what small glimpses would you be willing to share? How?

- *Remixing is a pathway toward transformation.* One word that Janelle uses at the beginning of her chapter is *remix.* What a wonderful way to contextualize the adaptation, improvisation, and modification of teaching that we do from one moment, or day, to another. For understanding the way classroom practices are continually adapting and evolving, the concept of remixing is a useful metaphor for the reconfiguring of practices and then distributing them—to our students and learning community, as well as to our broader professional online learning community.

  Questions to consider: What aspects of your teaching practice are most ripe to be remixed? How might shifts transform your pedagogy in ways that make literacy learning ever more equitable?

- *Change matters.* Janelle powerfully highlights a significant leap in her teaching career and the ways this change positively affected her work, her outlook on her career, and her comfort level in revealing her practice to others. Such changes can be daunting, and personal circumstances and commitments may prohibit you from switching school sites, shifting contexts, or otherwise making "big" changes. However, Janelle expresses the feelings of rejuvenation she experienced from making and signaling new directions in her work.

Questions to consider: In what short-term and long-term ways can you try changing up your teaching practice? How might such changes affect the work you do and your perspective on teaching? How might you share the idea that "change matters" as a part of your advocacy?

- *Don't overly complicate it.* You may not fancy yourself a Twitter-savvy individual. That's fine. We hope you notice that, while clearly crafted to build on the conventions of Twitter, Janelle's examples (tweets) are not difficult pieces of media to produce. She happens to use this digital tool to highlight and help reveal the contexts of learning in her classroom. Twitter may be the vehicle for her advocacy, but Janelle is the driver.

  Questions to consider: What social media tools do you already use? How can you share with your existing online community of colleagues, friends, and family to help grow the number of stakeholders involved in your work?

Janelle makes a powerful declaration in this chapter: "Public education is about using transparency, collaboration, and reflection to inform our teaching and our learning." Janelle reminds us of the powerful, political stance that she—and hopefully you, the reader—takes in sharing her work with an audience beyond the walls of her classroom and school. These simple acts of transforming school walls into windows center advocacy on the profession, on student literacy learning, and on ourselves as teachers, seeking to grow and to thrive.

PART III

Centering Advocacy in English Teacher Education

There is too much at stake in U.S. education to simply hope that teachers will naturally acquire the acumen for advocacy. Fortunately, we have had the opportunity to learn from and share the voices of teacher educators who are—today—instilling the principles of everyday advocacy into their work with preservice and practicing teachers. In this section, we build on the enthusiasm and passion for advocacy that teachers in the previous section brought to bear on the lives of their students. In the chapters that follow, we hear how ELA teacher educators and teacher leaders are transforming their practices—and the training of the teaching field—through engaging in localized models of everyday advocacy. Every chapter in this section is written by teacher educators and is based on specific examples of how they've taken principles of everyday advocacy into their classrooms and professional learning settings to help teachers—new and experienced—begin to see advocacy as part of their professional identities. Because we believe sharing their stories is more useful than us offering you hollow guidance on what we think you should be doing, we have framed this section of the book as a prolonged conversation among some of the teacher educators we are privileged to learn with and from. At the same time, we know that there are often barriers to implementing these principles, whether time constraints, unwilling partnering schools, or colleagues' opinions that this form of advocacy exceeds the expectations of what *should* be taught within a teacher education program. Through the following pragmatic examples of what other teacher educators are doing, we present a variety of ways your colleagues across the country are integrating smart, safe, sustainable, and savvy advocacy approaches into teacher education in their local contexts, and we invite you to enter into conversations about the value of this approach.

In the seven chapters in this section, we share the work of teacher educators who are going beyond traditional coursework and assignments to create space in their curricula and pedagogy to introduce preservice teachers to everyday advocacy as well as those who are focusing on ways of integrating everyday advocacy into the lives of practicing teachers. We invited these teacher educators to write about an approach, strategy, or assignment they use in their undergraduate methods, graduate level classes, or other settings to promote teacher advocacy. We asked them to share both the large ideas that ground their approach to advocacy, as well as the pragmatics for how they carry it out. Thus, you will see specific examples of what these teacher educators have done, why they have done it, and how those with whom they work have responded.

In expanding the dialogue of this book to include these voices, we describe below some of the educational research that these educators are contributing to. We also frame the responsibilities of teacher educators and programs and pedagogical responsibilities: it is not enough to simply talk up activities like everyday advocacy. Instead, we highlight how such work must be embedded—as a form of praxis—in the instruction in teacher education courses.

Bridging Two Worlds

Building on the research of Feiman-Nemser and Buchmann (1985), Athanases, Caret, and Meyer (1992) describe the perils of the "two-worlds pitfall" that too frequently afflicts preservice teachers. This pitfall, they note, is, "the experience of feeling such tension between the concerns of academic learning at the university and the learning in action of the school that the world of the university tends to evaporate" (p. 36).

If you've spent time working in teacher education programs over the past three decades, this pitfall is an all too familiar one. We recognize this two-worlds pitfall as much more than simply a theoretical reading of the disconnect that some students experience during the months they are student teaching. Instead, we recognize— and have seen—how some students struggle to make connections between the theories taught in teacher education programs and the day-to-day realities of maintaining a sense of understanding and composure within a classroom. Working with adolescents (whether for the first or the thirtieth time) can feel overwhelming and intimidating, and in the moments that things feel on the brink of chaos, knowing how to interpret and act on the theories of teacher education can feel impossible.

Yet, as several of the contributors in this part of the book describe, it is precisely through the learning opportunities related to everyday advocacy that some preservice teachers thrive. We do not mean that this is a panacea for the discombobulation of becoming a teacher. However, because everyday advocacy can support what happens in classrooms, illuminate allies in moving forward, and illustrate the multi-dimensional aspects of being a teacher, we think there is a lot to be gained by using everyday advocacy to bridge the gap between the two worlds of teacher preparation.

Scrolling through the social media pages of many of our friends and colleagues, we see a consistent and inspiring commitment to the literacy practices of young people. Echoing the themes of several chapters in this book, many of the teachers we know amplify the ways they think about, work toward improving, and generally advocate from *within* their classrooms. These forms of vocal participation—from new and veteran teachers alike—are vulnerable forms of sharing and engagement (perhaps reverberating the theme of Janelle Bence's chapter in the previous section). In fact, many of the chapters in this section, including the contributions by Amber Jensen (Chapter 9), Jennifer Dail and Shelbie Witte (Chapter 10), and Robin Fuxa (Chapter 14), provide examples of how new teachers are brought into the habits of everyday advocacy in authentic and sustainable contexts. Building on students' interest in local politics, schooling experiences, and social media use, the chapters in this section respect the existing knowledge and expertise of new teachers and leverages these assets for powerful approaches to redefining teacher identities.

Finding Time and Space for Everyday Advocacy

Sure, you may be thinking to yourself, *this everyday advocacy stuff is nice, but can I really do this with my preservice teachers? With practicing teachers? How would I ever find the time?*

As teacher educators ourselves, we completely understand how thinly stretched our time with teacher candidates can be. Eking out even an extra day in one teacher education class to emphasize something that may not be reflected on high-stakes requirements of licensure programs can often feel impossible. Further, as licensure requirements vary from state to state, there's no single pathway for surreptitiously weaving something like everyday advocacy into the knotted pathways of teacher education programs. We fully understand that teacher educators often feel the way many new teachers do—that their time is squeezed to its limit in their K–12 classrooms—making deeply ingrained instruction around everyday advocacy seem impossible.

The same is true for the graduate classes we teach for practicing teachers—the time we seem able to spend with these teachers once they are in the classroom seems too-limited. Yet we know how important it is to provide support for these teachers, especially given the number who are leaving the profession and the despair that hangs over the heads of far too many teachers who choose to stay.

While we admire how some of the voices in this section are deeply creative in the ways they integrate advocacy into their courses, we believe that teachers must learn a stance of everyday advocacy in teacher education as intentionally as possible. If our responsibility as teacher educators is to prepare reflexive educators who can sustain agentic choices that are in the best interests of their students and of the teaching profession, knowing how to push for powerful, expansive forms of literacy instruction and learning must lead the way. This recognition leads to what we believe is a key shift in how secondary ELA methods courses might be framed. Instead of viewing everyday advocacy as something extra that you might attend to (if you have time), we think that advocacy can lead how you approach teaching methods courses. When your preservice teachers are learning the principles of instructional design or the theories of reading instruction or of rubric-based assessment, the core components that undergird the forms of advocacy described in this book are present: you are helping these teachers understand how and why to implement equitable and—hopefully—justice-driven instructional work. These efforts reflect the three core principles we described in this book's introduction— the importance of stories, of framing, and of situational context when engaging in an issue. As you read the chapters that follow, consider how the teacher educators in this section build implicitly from these principles.

As we prepare preservice teachers and support practicing teachers to make clear decisions, we need to include conversations around how to articulate and defend the pedagogical choices they are making. These discussions teach the principles of everyday advocacy, which then becomes ingrained in how teachers see the work they do at every step of their program and beyond. Instead of setting aside a day or a week to focus on literacy-centered advocacy, integration highlights that speaking knowledgeably about what our students need and ensuring that they are getting it is a fundamental component of the responsibilities of being a teacher.

A Reminder About What Teacher Educators *Do*

As we move forward in this volume, we want to state the obvious: teacher educators *are* teachers. So while we emphasize the ways that teacher educators are integrating everyday advocacy in their lessons and workshops and teacher groups (and hope that you can adapt these ideas, as well as contribute to the conversation), being an advocate for literacy and pedagogical decisions is not simply something we convey in higher education. It is something we must do, too.

Modeling pedagogy, demonstrating situated models of learning, and classroom advocacy—the goal of teacher education is not just about teaching these ideas to our teacher candidates and practicing teachers, it is about reinvigorating this work as expert educators who bring passion and knowledge to the ways we develop and teach our courses. Every lesson plan in our teacher education classes is an opportunity to model and intentionally name the activities, moves, and stances that shape how we teach. When you have engaged in forms of everyday advocacy outside a methods class or through an activity that a student experiences, name these occasions so that you can make explicit the nearly constant ways you structure courses for the teacher candidates you work with. The work we do as everyday advocates in our teacher education classrooms is no less than transformative, as it helps define anew what being a teacher means today. As you read these chapters, consider the tools you use in classrooms and beyond: *How can you use social media more intentionally? How can we work alongside parents and local stakeholders? What are the moments of learning and engagement that you can name and clearly label for new teachers to visualize what advocacy looks like in situ?*

Considering the history of teacher education, the rise of high-stakes assessment over several decades, and the related pressures on teacher education to meet these high-stakes demands in already packed programs, the complex identities of our preservice teachers are often overlooked when schools design and structure opportunities for preparing them to become teachers. Becoming a teacher in the third decade of the twenty-first century means something substantially different for our candidates than it might have meant in the years and decades past. Sustaining the act of being a teacher has shifted, as well. For example, the majority of new teachers today—assuming they attended U.S. public schools shortly before attending their undergraduate institutions—experienced K–12 schooling entirely in the era of No Child Left Behind accountability. Even though the Every Student Succeeds Act (ESSA) is in place as we write this today, this era of accountability and evaluation has been part of a decades-long push toward restrictive forms of literacy instruction and evaluation. The day-to-day and year-to-year differences are slight. However, looking at what students experience today compared to a generation or two ago, we acknowledge that the design and accountability for ELA classrooms is different.

Schools are constantly changing. Just as the world around us is reshaping our cultural practices and identities, so too are we reshaping those things that we have taken for granted in classrooms. Everyday advocacy can help us expand the possibilities and imagination of our field. When we push for teachers to see themselves as innovators and to refuse the limited assumptions of what happens in English classrooms, we are collectively pushing to broaden what our classrooms can mean and what we think teachers and students alike can do. Likewise, for each form of restrictive interpretation of what counts as reading and writing, everyday advocacy can highlight alternatives. Working within the system, we also want to recognize the possibilities of praxis—a pedagogy that embraces everyday advocacy is one that connects what students may be seeing in their placements. Instead of accepting the narrow forms of reading accountability simply because the publisher's program has been adopted by a school's district, everyday advocacy means equipping students to recognize the deeply literate practices at the heart of youth interests and harnessing these interests.

Finally, we want to recognize that much of the time spent in teacher education courses is focused on tools to ensure that teachers thrive in the day-to-day tumult of classroom instruction. And that makes a lot of sense! At the same time, we hope that teacher educators will also convey that being a teacher is about so much more than the what occurs in classrooms. Alongside mentors and facilitators of powerful learning, we are public intellectuals, entrusted to make clear decisions for our classrooms, as well as participants in a broader labor movement. Everyday advocacy illuminates that being a teacher comprises so much more than solely what happens within a classroom. And while the model we describe in this volume emphasizes advocacy for what happens in our classrooms, we believe it also can lead teachers toward various pathways of organizing and supporting justice at all levels of education and society.

In light of these different elements, we want to highlight that everyday advocacy can function as a reminder of why we do this work in the first place. The vast majority of us in teacher education left K–12 classrooms and entered this alternate space of instruction—teaching teachers. Our interests are aligned with improving the outcomes and livelihoods of both teachers and students in their classrooms. On any given day, we—Cathy and Antero—have found ourselves in the navel-gazing quandary wondering if the work we do in the hallowed ivory tower of academia makes any kind of difference in the schools and classrooms we left behind.

Acknowledging the myriad forms of privilege afforded to us in higher education settings, we take seriously our role in guiding approaches to everyday advocacy for and with classroom teachers. Improving and guiding the agentic opportunities of new teachers is one of the most important ways that we tip the scales of public education ever closer toward equity.

Walking the Walk

As teacher educators, we often experience the same kind of accountability pressure that our student teachers do. We must consider ourselves as capable of engaging in everyday advocacy as our teacher candidates are. We, too, need to walk the everyday advocacy walk, not simply speak to its virtues. This may feel uncomfortable. Particularly in the context in which we write this—with the substantial imbalance of power in how schools of education are staffed and the labor of contingent faculty that may be taken for granted by many institutions. There are important elements of political advocacy that need to be taken up but are beyond the scope of this book. However, even with this caveat, teacher educators generally have much more power than secondary teachers and eminently more power than our preservice students. We need to demonstrate that we are aware of these power differences and build off of the affordances advanced degrees and certificates provide us in terms of social capital and help us better facilitate forms of everyday advocacy. Making these gestures transparent connotes allyship with our teachers—both new and practicing—who may be uncomfortable testing the limits of their voices as advocates.

Looking Forward

Though we will introduce each chapter separately, we want to mention a few key themes from these powerful contributors. With regard to time being (or feeling) limited, the flexibility demonstrated by these contributors is an important component for educators to consider. For both secondary and higher-education classrooms, navigating the challenges of where, when, and with whom is a formidable task. Any successful approach to implementation must include flexibility: you'll need to sway to the rhythms and needs of others. This work is not simply about acknowledging and working toward common ground with others, it requires building trust and maintaining caring relationships. Proximally, this requires concern for the needs of partners, students, and other school members. Distally, too, it requires a deep caring for the teaching profession and—most importantly—for the young people that we are, ultimately, working to support.

It shouldn't be a surprise, by this point in the book, that these different approaches are implicitly and explicitly linked to the four S's of everyday advocacy. We call some of these out, specifically, in the coming chapters. However, we want to (again) reiterate that these teacher educators build localized visions of everyday advocacy in ways that are smart, safe, savvy, and sustainable.

Finally, as you read the chapters that follow, we encourage you to reflect on the following questions:

- What everyday advocacy practices does the author convey in their chapter? What led to these emphases?
- What are the contexts and conditions for everyday advocacy in these spaces? Does the chapter focus on in-class, extracurricular, hybrid, or other spaces for building toward everyday advocacy?
- What is adaptable? Knowing we all customize our instruction and our instructional designs, what components can you build on? What warning signs can you imagine? What theories of learning are reinforced?
- What might *your* next step be in implementing the practices of everyday advocacy in your teaching context?

References

Athanases, S.Z., Caret, E., Meyer, T. (1992). Four against "The two-worlds pitfall": University-schools collaboration in teacher education. *English Education*, *24*(1), 34–51.

Feiman-Nemser, S., & Buchmann, M. (1985). Pitfalls of experience in teacher preparation. *Teachers College Record*, *87*(1), 53–65.

Chapter 9

"But We're Not the Experts Yet"

Preservice Teachers Build a Foundation for Everyday Advocacy

Amber Jensen

Amber Jensen is a former high school teacher and an assistant professor at Brigham Young University. When she wrote this chapter, she was a graduate student at George Mason University where she thought deeply about how to help preservice teachers become more comfortable with advocacy. Here, she challenges us to find ways to incorporate advocacy, program-wide, into teacher education programs.

A few semesters ago, I had the opportunity to work with preservice teachers in a teacher research class that is the capstone of their master's program in secondary education at George Mason University. The course is grounded in principles of teacher action research (Goodnough, 2001; MacLean & Mohr, 1999) and teacher self-study (Lassonde, Galman, & Koskik, 2009; Samaras & Freese, 2006). Its purpose is to help new teachers develop practice-based research skills, including identifying and using research literature alongside classroom data to be able to answer their own professional inquiries and thus improve their teaching practice. For the culminating assignment of this course, preservice teachers are required to compose a research paper tied to a semester-long, teacher-led inquiry project. Writing a long-form academic research paper fulfills an important aspect of graduate education—situating students as new scholars within discourses in their field—and aims to professionalize new teachers as practitioner researchers.

By this point in their academic careers, writing a paper for a teacher and presenting key findings to peers in class have become predictable genres and contexts for creating and sharing knowledge. For this reason, the structure of the IMRaD-style research paper (Introduction, Methods, Results, and Discussion) was relatively familiar in terms of genre and audience, though reasonably complex in the process of research and analysis. (See Figure 9.1 for a description of each required component of the assignment.) While the preservice teachers struggled at first to identify meaningful research questions, to develop data collection methodologies, and to consider questions of validity and reliability, they mostly found direction as they worked together as peers and followed an assignment rubric as a roadmap to navigating their research and writing concerns.

Figure 9.1. Teacher Research Project Assignment Description

Assignment description modified from George Mason University Secondary Education Program's EDUC 695 Research in Secondary Education Assignment Description and Assessment Rubric.

Assignment Component	Assignment Component Description
Introduction	Briefly describe the setting, including the community, school, students, and other relevant information related to your teaching context. What is the purpose of your study? What problem or issue are you addressing? Describe why the concerns are important to you and what your research might help you learn as a result of its conduct. What is (are) your research question(s)? What is your hypothesis and how did you formulate it?
Literature Review	To adequately give context to and ground your own investigation in existing research related to your inquiry, cite and synthesize a minimum of ten (10) sources, at least half of which are from peer-reviewed journals from the past ten years, and discuss how they informed your research question(s) and study design. Beyond summarizing and drawing connections between the relevant research studies and theories you include, you should craft your literature review as a story of the study of your topic—as a dialogue between you and these other scholars, with a focus on what is and isn't known yet about your topic.

Assignment Component	Assignment Component Description
Methodology	Describe how you implemented your research, including the type of research approach you used. Include a description of subjects (i.e., students, teachers, administrators), the context of the research, the strategies and materials (put sample material in an appendix), the data collected, and a complete description of the data collection and analysis methodologies. Be sure to describe how you selected your methodology and design, what measures you took to assure the validity of your study, and how you triangulated your data. How did you analyze your data in light of your research question(s)?
Findings	Indicate what you discovered or found as a result of your data analysis. Focus on results that are related to your research concern and answer your research questions or shed light on your research hypotheses. Use illustrative examples from your data to show your findings. Remember that the goal is to share what you learned about your teaching for yourself first; our goal is not necessarily to extract findings that will be generalizable across teaching settings. Interpret your data in as much detail as possible, describing whether or not—or how—your findings corroborated your expectations. Were there any surprises in your findings? Can you think of alternative explanations for your findings?
Discussion	Reflect on the findings of your data collection and discuss what they might mean to you as a teacher and teacher researcher. What did you learn from the study? How will it influence your teaching—that is, based on the results and themes that emerged from the study, what changes will you make in your teaching? How will you share these findings with others? What are the implications for future research? Make some bold recommendations for how we might serve students better. Be sure to describe what all of this information—the teacher research process, your data, your findings—means to you as a professional and as a person. Describe potential implications of your study and its findings for other teachers, for teacher education, and/or for education policy makers.

The portion of the project that elicited the most distress among my students, however, was the Teacher Research Impact Presentation (see Figure 9.2 for a full description), which required preservice teachers to consider an audience for their research findings beyond me and their classmates. This key part of the assignment asked preservice teachers to share the impact of their teacher research with an audience in the real world who they think should care about their research findings. The preservice teachers struggled to identify audiences with whom they would feel confident sharing their results; one student protested, "We are supposed to make recommendations to other people about what does or doesn't work in teaching? But we're not the experts yet!" Their classmates nodded in agreement; the preservice teachers worried that, as novices, they were not yet in a position to offer suggestions to other teachers, especially those they viewed as seasoned experts.

Figure 9.2. Teacher Research Impact Presentation Assignment Description

Assignment description modified from George Mason University Secondary Education Program's EDUC 695 Research in Secondary Education course and program exit requirement description.

Teacher Research Impact Presentation: Working independently, you will identify an authentic, alternative, preferably contemporary, media-based method through which you will share the impact of your teacher research with an audience you care about and/or to an audience that you think should care about your teacher research results. While you will make a brief presentation of your individual research findings in class, the mission of this assignment is for you to design and enact a presentation that moves along the public's understanding of your study. You are encouraged to display and present these findings in a real-world setting and through creative means, with your primary goal being to demonstrate the significance of your research to a broader community. You may, potentially, share your project with faculty of the Secondary Program and members of the larger college or educational community as well.

As an English educator committed to fostering teachers' advocacy mindsets from the beginnings of their careers, I hoped this assignment would challenge preservice teachers to consider who (beyond me and their peers) might benefit from learning about their research and how they might frame their findings to "move along the public's understanding of the topic," as the assignment read. But this preservice teacher's reaction, a concern shared by her peers in the class, encapsulated a significant barrier to teacher advocacy, particularly for early-career teachers: the belief that their knowledge and experience aren't yet valid or valued. I wondered how we, as English educators, could establish a foundation for the next generation of teachers to see themselves as everyday advocates. What skills and dispositions do preservice teachers need to develop in order to claim a voice and to enact change? How can we use methods classes and field experiences as labs for practicing and enabling advocacy, even among new teachers?

In recent years, I have experimented with integrating advocacy foundations in three different phases of my work with graduate-level preservice English teachers at George Mason University: a methods course, student teaching, and the capstone teacher research course I mentioned above. Across all three settings, I have revised existing assignments and designed experiences to focus on helping preservice teachers construct beliefs, develop narratives, and share their knowledge in ways that might enable new possibilities in twenty-first century literacy instruction. My approach centers on theories of learning transfer (Nowacek, 2011), teacher discourses (McCarthey, Woodard, & Kang, 2014; Smagorinsky, Gibson, Bickmore, Moore, & Cook, 2004), and teacher agency (Biesta, Priestly, & Robinson, 2015; Kayi-Aydar, 2015; Priestley, Edwards, Priestly, & Miller, 2012). Taken together, these theories suggest that when teachers can metacognitively see—and articulate—their own theories and beliefs about literacy education, they will be more ready to rhetorically sell these beliefs in ways that may effect changes in practices and policies (Jensen, 2019a).

While it is impossible for me to promise preservice teachers that the beliefs they develop and the narratives they share will be always valued by public audiences, it is my goal to help them see their own knowledge as valid. I hope to help them frame theory- and practice-based narratives strategically and to share them with others in ways that will lead to positive change. In the Teacher Research Impact Presentation assignment and at all points of my interaction with preservice teachers in their teacher preparation, I hope to help preservice teachers see themselves as everyday advocates.

In the remainder of this chapter, I share how I have begun to integrate the building blocks of everyday advocacy into my work with preservice teachers across three sites of learning: a teaching methods course, student teachng, and a teacher research course. I support preservice teachers in developing an advocacy approach to teaching by helping them situate their identities, identify audiences, develop and name theories and beliefs, and practice advocacy as they communicate their learning in public and authentic ways.

English Methods Course: Situating Identities and Identifying Audiences

In an English teaching methods course, I invited preservice teachers to reflect on how their own identities and learning experiences shape their views on education, literacy, and their futures as teachers. In class discussions and written reflections, I prompted them to interrogate these views alongside the practices they see in schools—practices such as teaching formulaic essay writing, measuring student understanding using reading check quizzes, and teaching from a library of novels representing a limited canon. Beyond asking them to situate themselves within these practices as former K–12 students and as future K–12 teachers, I asked a question to help them practice advocacy in action: "What role does digital writing play in the ELA classroom?"

In a simulated debate, the preservice teachers imagined how various stakeholders in a school setting might respond to this question. Then, acting in a range of roles (e.g., a colleague, a parent, a student, an administrator), the preservice teachers role-played a debate in which they responded to each other's arguments. The activity required them to consider the priorities and pressures each stakeholder brings to such a conversation. It challenged them to frame an issue and present a response to imagined audiences from varied perspectives (for more discussion about the debate and its impact on preservice teacher learning, see Jensen, 2019b). As preservice teachers identified their reasons for the digital writing practices they advocated, they began to assess institutions and policies and identify allies as well as barriers to change. Though it was just a simulation, the debate seemed to be a useful foundation to help preservice teachers position themselves as advocates, worthy of contributing to real-world discourses beyond the methods classroom, in ways that could shape their teaching.

Student Teaching: Developing Theories and Naming Practices

Imagining audiences is not enough, however. I noticed during the methods class that the preservice teachers struggled to articulate *why* they held the beliefs they did about twenty-first century literacy instruction. They knew working with multimodal texts was important, for example, but when it came time to justifying that choice against pressures of standardized tests or statewide curricula, the narratives they drew on—narratives about what is most engaging for students—were not likely to stand up against policy language based in learning outcomes or college readiness. During a student teaching semester, then, I piloted an intervention with four student teachers in middle and high schools that was designed to help them develop—and become comfortable talking about—frameworks for twenty-first century literacies in their own words: what counts as writing, what kinds of writing practices are most important, and what teaching practices best engage students with these meaningful genres and practices.

Over five interviews, wherein preservice teachers drew on their teaching experiences to develop a working conception of twenty-first century writing, I found that each preservice teacher not only developed nuanced and theory-supported conceptions but also became more comfortable talking about their beliefs, noticing where classroom practices, institutional policies, and public narratives did and did not manifest these beliefs in action. Situating this intervention during their student teaching semester allowed them to reflect on teaching tensions to determine what might be possible in future classrooms and what institutional structures might help or hinder them. One of the preservice teachers said: the series of interviews "made me reflect on how I want [to be] true to myself and push the envelope a little bit in terms of what has existed in my school and what I want to be able to do." Because of the ways our conversations helped her center her own values, this preservice teacher felt more confident to become an advocate when opportunities to propose and enact practices that aligned with her teaching beliefs arose (Jensen, 2020).

What I learned from these interviews convinced me that preservice teachers need more opportunities to develop their own frameworks for theories and practices that support twenty-first century literacies if they are to be ready to engage as advocates in public conversations about these practices. Metacognitive opportunities can happen in conversation with mentor teachers, with university supervisors, with peers in a student teaching seminar. The key is to implement opportunities for preservice teachers to develop their own frameworks and practice using narratives that will be familiar and impactful in authentic, real-world conversations with public audiences and decision-makers.

Teacher Research Course: Practicing Acts of Advocacy

Finally, in addition to understanding audiences and developing narratives, the assignment I described at the beginning of this chapter challenged preservice teachers to engage in public discourse around their own teacher research. Helping them explore current discourses around issues relevant to their own teaching sites and teaching practices helped them frame their learning in ways that matter beyond the teacher research course itself. The preservice teachers in my teacher research course researched literacy pedagogies such as student-centered grammar instruction, independent reading programs, and student choice in writing experiences. They engaged in the academic discourses surrounding these topics, finding relevant research and grounding theirs in current literature in the field. They wrote extended research papers on these topics. But they also practiced real-world advocacy by identifying relevant audiences with whom they shared their findings in ways that were likely to begin to shift public understanding. The preservice teachers shared their research with their coteachers, team teachers, collaborative learning teams, and wider networks of teacher colleagues beyond their schools. Some shared their findings with the students represented in their studies. One preservice teacher shared her research with her principal, who shared a digital file of her presentation with the entire faculty. The teacher impact presentations were delivered in formal presentations, in team planning meetings, via ongoing conversations, and in other ways the preservice teachers deemed most authentic and useful.

Regarding the experience of translating their research into narratives relevant for wider audiences, many of the preservice teachers reported being surprised at how well their findings were received by their colleagues and administrators and students. One preservice teacher said her colleagues were surprised to learn what she discovered about how students experience forgiveness in the classroom, prompting reflection on their own classroom management practices; another reported that her research presentation prompted her teaching team to identify new ways to consider students' linguistic ability when designing lessons and evaluating common assessments. Two preservice teachers found their audiences to be sympathetic with the challenges uncovered by their research, and one said the veteran teacher with whom she shared her research drew on 30 years of experience to help evaluate her conclusions. While at first, the preservice teachers in this course conveyed reluctance to position themselves as experts, their experience of framing and sharing their research with a range of real-world audiences seemed to build their confidence as teaching professionals, foster productive professional conversations, and prompt new considerations and evaluations of teaching practices in their existing professional communities.

Final Thoughts and Next Steps

So how might we enable advocacy without putting an undue burden on new teachers who are all at once navigating new identities and just beginning to develop their beliefs and practices? How might we help preservice teachers feel more confident in the expertise they are developing as teachers and as voices for literacy education in the twenty-first century?

First, we must lower the stakes for what "counts" as advocacy. Start small. For example, we can work with student teachers to practice pitching a new assignment idea or classroom routine to their mentor teacher, encouraging the student teachers to draw on relevant research in the field and articulate their own teaching values and beliefs. These discussions can extend eventually to team teachers, professional learning communities, and even entire departments as opportunities arise. Often, advocacy work begins when teachers find allies, so we can prompt preservice teachers to practice talking about their teaching practices and beliefs with parents, to partner with like-minded teachers, and to share their successes with administrators. Finding colleagues with more institutional power or strategic knowledge may be a way to expand conversations and foster changes. Helping preservice teachers identify audiences and practice sharing their narratives may be one of the best investments in preservice teacher education because these strategies will enable teachers to see themselves as contributors to meaningful discourses beyond the academic conversations of teacher education programs.

Second, we should facilitate metacognition throughout teacher education programs—in coursework, in field work, in student teaching—to help preservice teachers develop strong foundations in the reasons their work matters, participate in the conversations that exist, and gain the confidence to propose specific and actionable next steps for improving literacy education. These conversations may be integrated into regular debriefs with university supervisors during student teaching, into discussion boards with peers, or into seminar courses designed for reflection on teaching field-experiences. They may take the form of rationale statements accompanying a lesson plan or unit plan in a methods course or the form of a statement of teaching beliefs and values composed at the beginning of a teacher education program and revisited and revised at various points along the way. It is important that we help preservice teachers know more than just how to *perform* teaching; they need to develop knowledge and be able to talk about *how* and *why* they teach the way they do.

Finally, we need to pair course and field experiences with authentic assignments through which preservice teachers can practice writing for "real" audiences. For example, they might compose a letter to the editor, write a blog post for other educators, engage in a Twitter conversation, draft a letter to parents for curriculum preview, or develop a proposal to an administrator. Just as K–12 students benefit from writing in real-world genres and for authentic audiences, preservice teachers will gain confidence as they practice communicating with real audiences in real ways.

Building a foundation for advocacy into preservice teachers education is just an entry point. I hope preservice teachers will engage in lasting participation in public discourse with other engaged practitioners and change makers. Rather than seeing themselves as novices, I hope they will see themselves as advocates and public intellectuals, ready to contribute to and improve the wider conversations surrounding their profession and their practice.

What We Noticed as We Read This Chapter

What does teacher expertise look like, and how do we cultivate it in the new teachers entering our profession? Considering that teacher leadership efforts often focus on veteran teachers who have honed leadership over years of experience, Amber Jensen's exploration of the development of expertise in *new* teachers is long overdue. Further, in seeing how teachers bring this expertise—and a broader recognition of it—to bear on issues of advocacy, Amber adeptly foregrounds the "smart" components of teacher expertise within the formal coursework of teacher education programs.

Perhaps more explicitly than other chapters in this section, Amber's chapter illustrates *how* to integrate elements of teacher advocacy into the foundation of teacher education programs. This is a key opportunity for all readers of this book. Current teacher educators, we encourage you to look at and consider adapting your assignments and prompts. Current educators who may not work in higher education, these school-based prompts can function as your own, interest-driven form of professional development. Reviewing the lessons that Amber shares, we are reminded that instruction in her context includes many approaches that will look familiar in secondary English language arts classrooms as well. For example, she encourages her preservice teachers to develop meaningful research questions and a plan for fully exploring and answering these questions, which looks strikingly familiar to the kinds of project-based approaches that are often taught in secondary English classrooms. Though the methodologies may shift, Amber subtly highlights the parallels between the experiences of secondary classroom teachers and educators in preservice teacher education programs. As we look at the moves that Amber describes, we want to note three themes in her chapter.

- *Starting small.* Amber describes structures to help preservice teachers start small and set the stakes of advocacy in ways that are manageable. This slow, snowball-like approach to generating momentum for teachers over time is one way that teacher confidence can be tied to feelings and validation of teacher expertise.

  Questions to consider: What are some small ways you could start introducing advocacy in your own teacher education program or the professional learning experiences you lead? What might be your first steps?

- *Developing a knowledge base.* Amber notes that "when teachers can metacognitively see—and articulate—their own theories and beliefs about literacy education, they will be more ready to rhetorically sell these beliefs in ways that may effect changes in practices and policies." When teachers learn more about the theoretical underpinnings of literacy (through methods classes, experiences, and conversations with others), they gain confidence and are thus better able to talk to others. Throughout the chapter, Amber demonstrates how she helps her own preservice teachers work in ways that are smart.

  Questions to consider: How do you already introduce important theories of literacy and learning to your preservice or practicing teachers? How might you add an advocacy twist to that?

- *Scaffolding advocacy experiences program-wide.* Amber reminds us that new teachers have relatively few opportunities for speaking to (and advocating in) the "real world." By creating a series of invitations and assignments for preservice teachers across three separate courses, she shows us how advocacy can build across a whole teacher education program, helping students gain confidence in their expertise and their ability to communicate their expertise to others.

Questions to consider: Think about the sequence of courses in your teacher education program or professional learning experiences that you lead. How might you consider scaffolding advocacy through those courses or experiences?

Across the board, Amber Jensen's chapter speaks to teachers not simply as capable of interpreting and explaining research but also as being critical theorists. Amber strives for her preservice teachers to see their own knowledge as valid, and we think the guidelines she provides can function as an approach for *all* educators. Owning our literacy expertise and wielding it for change are concepts that we hope readers extrapolate across the entire ecology of schooling in the United States.

References

Biesta, G., Priestley, M., & Robinson, S. (2015). The role of beliefs in teacher agency. *Teachers and Teaching, 21*(6), 624–640.

Goodnough, K. (2001). Teacher development through action research. *Action in teacher Education, 23(1),* 37–46.

Jensen, A. (2019a). Fostering preservice teacher agency in 21st century writing instruction. *English Teaching: Practice and Critique, 18(2).*

Jensen, A. (2019b). Writing in and for the 21st century: Crossing digital and multimodal thresholds in EL methods courses. In H. L. Hallman, K. Pastore-Capuana, & D. L. Pasternak (Eds.), *Using tension as a resource: New visions in teaching the English language arts methods class* (pp. 59–71). London, England: Rowman & Littlefield.

Jensen, A. (2020). Writing in and for the 21st Century: Crossing digital and multimodal thresholds in ELA methods courses. Manuscript submitted for publication.

Kayi-Aydar, H. (2015). Teacher agency, positioning, and English language learners: Voices of preservice classroom teachers. *Teaching and Teacher Education, 45,* 94–103.

Lassonde, C. A., Galman, S., & Kosnik, C. (Eds.). (2009). *Self-study research methodologies for teacher educators.* Rotterdam, Netherlands: Sense.

MacLean, M. S., & Mohr, M. (1999). *Teacher-researchers at work.* Berkeley, CA: The National Writing Project.

McCarthey, S. J., Woodard, R., & Kang, G. (2014). Elementary teachers negotiating discourses in writing instruction. *Written Communication, 31*(1), 58–90.

Nowacek, R. (2011). *Agents of integration: understanding transfer as a rhetorical act.* Carbondale, IL: Southern Illinois University Press.

Priestley, M., Edwards, R., Priestley, A., & Miller, K. (2012). Teacher agency in curriculum making: Agents of change and spaces for manoeuvre. *Curriculum Inquiry, 42*(2), 191–214.

Samaras, A. P., & Freese, A. R. (2006). *Self-study of teaching practices primer.* New York, NY: Peter Lang.

Smagorinsky, P., Gibson, N., Bickmore, S. T., Moore, C. P., & Cook, L. S. (2004). Praxis shock: Making the transition from a student-centered university program to the corporate climate of schools. *English Education, 36*(3), 214–245.

Chapter 10

"A Practice of Passion"

Advocacy in Online Spaces

Jennifer S. Dail and Shelbie Witte
(with Linda Latuszek, Victoria Thompson, and Adam Watson)

Jennifer Dail, lead author of this piece, is a professor at Kennesaw State University. Though she writes in the first person, she is ever mindful of her long partnership with Shelbie Witte, a professor at Oklahoma State University, who contributed heavily to the ideas brought forth in this chapter about the connections between advocacy and a digital presence and how preservice teachers learn to use online spaces to advocate for digital approaches to teaching. Linda Latuszek, Victoria Thompson, and Adam Watson are three of those preservice teachers.

As a teacher educator situated in the southeastern United States for my entire career, advocacy has not been a word I have used to describe the stances I take both personally and professionally and, therefore, has not been a word I have used with my students until recently. Simply put: in the South, the word *advocacy* implies a certain type of person—one who is loud and pushy and who always has an agenda. Yet, as I began to recognize the ways in which my own work as a teacher educator is indeed advocacy, I started looking for spaces to bring the concept into my teaching, to share it with preservice teacher candidates.

The blog *Teaching Sam and Scout* (2014) proposes defining advocacy as "a practice of passion." The author goes on to say, "advocacy is the work that we do for the issues that keep us up at night and the issues that get us out of bed in the morning. The work of advocacy might be participating in a political conversation with a formal organization, but it also might be . . . casual conversation in the hallway about an issue that makes us come alive" (para. 3) In using this definition, I saw a space to meet students who may not yet see themselves as advocates for the teaching profession. Additionally, in my work with preservice teachers, my colleague Shelbie Witte and I saw a space to introduce my students to and engage them in advocacy through online platforms such as social media or blogs.

Positioning the Work With Students

In the summer of 2019, I began teaching an online digital media and technology course for English language arts (ELA) teachers in the Master of Arts in Teaching program at Kennesaw State University. The students in the class were newly enrolled in the program and would not enter their year-long field experiences until fall 2019, the next semester. The course asks not only that students tinker with technology and digital media applications in the ELA classroom, but also that they enter into professional conversations in public online spaces and consider what participating publicly in online spaces means to them as teachers and what it might mean to the students with whom they will work.

In considering the broader context of the course and positioning my students as advocates within teaching communities, I had reached out to Shelbie, founding director of the Initiative for 21st Century Literacies Research (http://www.initiativefor21 research.org). The initiative builds "upon faculty and graduate student research on contemporary literacies people need to succeed in complex environments in and beyond schools" (Our Initiative, n.d.). The initiative positions itself as a larger platform for the type of advocacy work, grounded in research and exemplars, that I was asking my students to take up in my course. Shelbie invited me to submit exceptional student blog posts to the Initiative's blog, *Pedagogy in the 21st Century* (http://www.initiativefor21research .org/theory-to-practice-connections).

Within the context of the course, it made sense for students to develop blogs that focused on their work with technology and that looked forward to how they might critically situate technology to advocate for including it in particular ways in their field experience in the upcoming year and beyond, into their own classrooms. In other words, I asked them to use technology to advocate for technology use. Specifically, I asked students to consider their blog as an online makerspace intended to serve as a platform for their inquiry work with technology. I proposed to students that makerspaces not only offer a constructivist and constructionist space where students can work through ideas but also present a mindset that should be taught (Makerspace for Education, n.d.). Makerspaces offer a means to help students move beyond consumption of technology to creation with it. Within this framework, students might view their blogs as public advocacy not just for critical and purposeful technology integration but also for makerspaces as a means of supporting student inquiry. There is a growing advocacy for this type of work in schools and classrooms, and it is critical that teachers drive what learning looks like in their schools by "helping policy makers understand as we develop frameworks that move away from consumption, toward creation in our educational settings" (Makerspace for Education, n.d.).

The Assignment

I asked students to set up a free blog on WordPress.com and provided them with links to video and text tutorials for support. They were required to create an "About" page where they introduced themselves to readers in ways that were personal and that described why they were creating this blog (beyond a requirement for class) and their qualifications for sharing digital media and technology information. (They were also required to set up the home page by removing the pre-included example content on the template's page.)

I set up a shared table in Google Docs where students shared links to their blogs so they knew what blogs to follow based on our class. I also asked that they start following additional blogs as they came across them in their work over the course of the semester.

Now the students were ready for blogging, in which they created and maintained weekly content related to our course readings. The idea behind these weekly posts was to create a forum for them to tinker with technology by experimenting with various tools and platforms and to share that work as a model for our class, other teachers, and their students. I encouraged them to think about their upcoming teaching context and to create content that they could actually use with their students in the upcoming year. I also prescribed a format for their blog posts:

1. Tinker with a new technology. In other words, do not choose a platform or tool you are comfortable with and keep using it because it is quick and easy. Expand your breadth as a teacher and technology user.
2. Choose a technology that best illustrates the theories and practices about which we are reading. In other words, be intentional rather than choosing something because it is sexy and shiny.
3. Embed the work you have done in your post.
4. Write a reflection within the post that unpacks your thinking about the work, making explicit connections to our course readings and viewings. Those connections should be shared in APA format. You should also link to outside media and sources, as this is a primary affordance of a blog.

The reflection proved a critical component in the assignment as it allowed them to demonstrate their thinking even if their technology product fell short in some way (e.g., technical difficulties or not showing the ideas they aimed to show). It also offered a structure for creating a post for potential submission to the Initiative for 21st Century Literacies Research blog. I assigned the following components for their reflections, with suggestions for length in parentheses following each component:

1. An overview of what you are doing, including theories and practices you are addressing (a first introductory paragraph)
2. An overview of the technology and tools you are using (a second introductory paragraph)
3. An exploration of why these are the best tools for this maker project, including addressing their affordances and constraints (Jones & Hafner, 2012; 2–3 paragraphs)
4. A reflection of the role of this type of creative work in your classroom, connecting to the readings we have conducted in this blogging cycle (3–4 paragraphs)

The goal, in other words, was to have them (1) learn more about technologies and tools by using them; (2) reflect on their learning; and (3) take that learning public to advocate for the use of digital spaces in secondary classrooms.

Preservice Teachers' Thoughts on Advocacy

I invited some of my participating preservice teachers who had created strong blogs to reflect on advocacy and contribute their voices to this chapter to see how they were taking up thinking about this sort of public work as they moved into classrooms in the fall. The three preservice teachers I selected see themselves as advocates; however, I did not know they self-identified that way when I selected them. Linda, one of the teachers I selected, shared, "I envision someone who takes up advocacy work as an individual with purpose, passion, and commitment. I think that advocacy requires personal involvement in a cause and needs commitment so others know the advocate can be counted on to support and stand up for the cause. Advocates often give a voice to others who may not have the platform to be seen and heard." Adam defined "an advocate as someone who goes about the normal call of duty to push for not only change in their field but a continuous discussion about best practices concerning the people that they serve. Advocates are not satisfied with the status quo and seek to persuade those within their circles of influence that they should not be either." Victoria views advocacy and advocates in a similar manner but offers the following caveat: "It is not easy to be an advocate as a novice teacher because everything is so uncharted and there are *so* many things to prepare for and master and so little time." She does note, however, "I have certainly been able to practice educational advocacy in my time as a teacher thus far." Her advocacy practice took form first when she presented an instructional strategy at the National Council of Teachers of English Annual Convention and second as she shared instructional strategies and their effectiveness with both local and nonlocal colleagues through online platforms.

Potential for Online Platforms in Teacher Advocacy Work

These three preservice teachers view the potential of online platforms for advocacy as limitless, especially with an upcoming generation of teachers who grew up learning in online spaces. Adam believes "that these platforms can allow professionals to communicate with like-minded individuals beyond their own schools, and in doing so, isolation will be minimized and conversations will be pushed forward." He continues by musing, "Online platforms can serve as a way to organize robust ideas in an effective way that is accessible to teachers, students, parents, and stakeholders."

Victoria sees blogs as a means for teachers to share instructional approaches and create resources and conversation around them. In her work, she also "found that groups on Facebook, as well as educator profiles and hashtag groups on Instagram, are beneficial communities where teachers can connect and support one another, ask questions, provide solutions, and receive constructive feedback."

Moving forward into fall semester and seeing the positive response from the teacher candidates in my summer course, I developed a social media advocacy project for master of education students enrolled in my fall course. In working alongside Shelbie and her own students, I shifted from just seeing myself as an advocate to also considering myself responsible for priming students to take up everyday advocacy work in their own professional journeys.

What We Noticed as We Read This Chapter

Though digital tools have been used for production and action in nearly every project described in the past two sections of this book, Jennifer Dail and Shelbie Witte's explorations echo Kristen Strom's description in Chapter 5 of how she shares her classroom learning in online spaces as a form of advocacy, as well as the digital organization of Strom's writing group.

There is a powerful relationship between advocacy and technology in this chapter. Just as Amber Jensen's chapter (Chapter 9) explores the ways that teacher expertise must be cultivated, the ways that Jennifer and her students are "tinkering" with technology highlights an important recognition that we are always learning—and ideally *playing*—in deeply literate, digital contexts. We see in her efforts to cultivate this tinkering perspective among her students that some key advocacy moves are being made.

- *Advocacy is not a solo process.* By reaching out to her colleague (and coauthor) Shelbie and building off this relationship to highlight spaces and resources for exploration, Jennifer demonstrates the power of collaboration. She does the same for her students by introducing them to the idea of collaboration by sharing blogs first with each other and then with the larger community. Working with others to share and build ideas, to see that we're not alone in this work, is a vital component of advocacy.

Questions to consider: While Shelbie is a one of a kind member of the literacy research community, each of you works with and knows somebody who can support your work and connect you to additional people and resources. Who might those people be? How might you help your own students discover potential collaborators and allies?

- *Advocates build their knowledge of their issue.* By inviting her students to better understand multiple tools and technologies and to reflect on them, Jennifer asks them to develop their knowledge base, to work in ways that are smart. Knowing their topic so well that they could speak with others confidently and convincingly led them to go public in various ways, from their own blogs to presenting at a national conference to publishing on a national online platform.

Questions to consider: Whatever issue you, in your role as a teacher educator or leader, might ask your preservice and practicing teachers to focus on requires a knowledge base—on both your part and theirs. How might you help those you work with develop their expertise? If it's a shared question or issue, how might you provide resources? How might you help them find ways to develop their own resources? How might you open your class or workshop to a shared body of knowledge, especially through digital platforms?

- *An advocate consider themself an advocate.* Jennifer's opening reminds us that the term *advocate* carries several meanings—and not always ones that are positive: "Simply put," she explains, "in the South, the word *advocacy* implies a certain type of person—one who is loud and pushy, and who always has an agenda." Thus, helping students see themselves as advocates can be a complicated undertaking. Jennifer's approaches—an almost back-door introduction to advocacy—led the way to definitions that her students felt comfortable taking on: advocates are people who "are not satisfied with the status quo and seek to persuade those within their circles of influence that they should not be either" and those who "often give a voice to others who may not have the platform to be seen and heard."

Questions to consider: What are the connotations of the word *advocate* in your local context? What connotations do the preservice and practicing teachers with whom you work hold about the word? How might you find out? How might you disrupt, revise, or build upon current definitions?

References

Jones, R. H., & Hafner, C. A. (2012). *Understanding digital literacies: A practical intro-duction*. New York, NY: Routledge.

Makerspace for Education. (n.d.). Retrieved from http://www.makerspaceforeducation .com/makerspace.html

Our Initiative. (n.d.). Retrieved from http://www.initiativefor21research.org/our-initiative .html

Teaching Sam & Scout. (2014, November 25). Teacher advocacy: What is it and why should you care? (A Guest Post) [Web log post]. Retrieved from http://www.samandscout .com/teacher-advocacy-what-is-it-and-why-should-you-care-a-guest-post/

Chapter 11

Upcycling the edTPA

Practicing Rhetorical Argumentation and Advocacy through Teacher Performance Assessments

Christine M. Dawson and Anny Fritzen Case

Christine Dawson (Sienna College) and Anny Fritzen Case (Gonzaga University) teach teacher education and literacy courses to preservice teachers. In this chapter, they offer a window on how they help students reconsider the edTPA as a practice ground for advocacy, shifting the narrative surrounding this required assessment.

"U pcycling" may conjure images of a pair of old garden boots repurposed as a planter, or painted milk crates jigsawed into a clever coffee table. But how can we upcycle something like the edTPA, the preservice teacher assessment mandated by many college programs and state certification requirements? This chapter explores using teacher performance assessments as a practice ground on which preservice teachers can develop effective advocacy strategies.

The edTPA (Teacher Performance Assessment) is a high-stakes portfolio assessment that affects preservice teaching across the country through both the assessment itself and the trickle-down impact it has on curriculum and pedagogy in methods courses. Briefly, the edTPA—an assesement that grew out of a joint venture of the

Stanford Center for Assessment, Learning, and Equity (SCALE) and the American Association of Colleges of Teacher Education (AACTE)—requires that preservice teachers demonstrate their preparation to enact three core professional tasks: planning, instruction, and assessment. Candidates compile a portfolio that includes artifacts from their lesson planning (lesson plans, instructional materials, assessments), instruction (video clips), and assessments (student work samples), which they interpret by responding to specified prompts for each task, resulting in 20 to 30 pages of total written commentary. Directions for completing the edTPA are provided in subject-specific handbooks, and candidates upload their finished portfolios to a central website for scoring according to detailed rubrics.

As teacher educators, we have found that helping methods students navigate the edTPA is challenging, to say the least, especially while they are also immersed in the messy work of learning to teach. During student teaching, preservice teachers are actively building a repertoire of classroom practices, learning about their students and contexts, participating in their classroom communities, and taking on increasing instructional roles. When faced with the edTPA, preservice teachers also must gather data and assemble materials for an external audience, adding layers of complexity to their experience. For this reason (and others, which we talk about in this chapter), our field continues to grapple with the role of the edTPA in teacher education programs, questioning the way it can consume student teachers' time and thinking during their internship. Nevertheless, many colleges and universities use the edTPA as a program-level assessment, and many states (including our own) require teacher candidates to pass the edTPA to become certified. Thus, for many teacher candidates across the country edTPA is an immediate reality and high-stakes mandate they must face.

While the edTPA is, first and foremost, an assessment, we have deliberately "upcycled" the edTPA to help students learn strategies to analyze an audience, make and support evidence-based claims, garner support from research, and establish healthy professional boundaries. As teacher educators who work with candidates during their methods and student teaching semesters, our goal is to help our preservice teachers position themselves as advocates—for their students, their practice, and their own professional commitments. We hope our preservice teachers will use these advocacy skills long after their edTPA scores are forgotten.

Explicit Reframing: Positionality and Stance

Our own students, in New York and Washington, were among the first nationwide to face the edTPA as a requirement for state certification, and we've been helping students through the process since 2013. The anxiety surrounding the edTPA was palpable from the beginning, with students fearing a faceless assessor's power over their access to certification. Yet we were unwilling to engage in "test-prep" approaches, especially as we sought to model the kinds of instruction we hoped our preservice teachers would carry into their own classrooms. We began to frame the edTPA not as a test but as an *argument* that preservice teachers must make to advocate for their advancement and professional choices. We also foreground the need for teachers to find and raise their voices even when addressing a powerful audience.

Because the edTPA is a high-stakes licensure assessment, many preservice teachers naturally feel a sense of vulnerability when anticipating, preparing for, and actually writing the required materials. One of our goals, however, is to disrupt this positionality as a "vulnerable test taker." Instead, we emphasize that the edTPA is likely the first of many moments when our preservice teachers will be called to showcase their professional decisions. For better or for worse, teachers are subject to a myriad of evaluators, ranging from parents to administrators to National Board assessors. We recognize the vulnerability inherent in each of these situations, but we also emphasize the potential when teachers can *intentionally* frame their practice, for a given audience, in light of their own goals and commitments. We therefore invite our preservice teachers to analyze the difference between positioning themselves as test-takers and positioning themselves as emerging professionals. We collectively think about the rationale, characteristics, and implications of each position, as well as moments across their careers when they will have to make similar decisions.

Reading an Audience: Analyzing Priorities and Values

From a rhetorical standpoint, teachers interact with a wide variety of audiences: they prepare lessons to engage students, they communicate with families and guardians, they collaborate with colleagues, and they articulate priorities and decisions to administrators. Some of these audiences have considerable power in teachers' professional lives, evaluating performance and determining professional opportunities. Different audiences value and prioritize different things, so "reading" an audience can empower teachers to target their message more deliberately and proactively—a critical component of effective advocacy.

The edTPA offers preservice teachers an opportunity to practice interpreting an audience's values and priorities. Because the edTPA portfolios will be read and evaluated by external reviewers, the assessment handbooks provide specific commentary prompts and assessment rubrics to guide candidate submissions. While this information is useful from a test-taking perspective, we also work with our candidates to help them practice analyzing an audience. We ask them to analyze the language of the handbooks to help them infer the assumptions, beliefs, and values held by the designers and scorers. Thus, we begin with the assumption that the edTPA audience is *knowable* and that understanding an audience is critical for our work as advocates.

We start by noting that the edTPA audience prioritizes teachers' planning, instruction, and assessment, which form the foci for the central tasks. When our students then analyze the commentary prompts, we help them observe that each question represents information the edTPA audience particularly values. In Task 1 for example, the edTPA asks about the instructional focus of a lesson sequence, as well as how well this focus aligns with the planned teaching/learning strategies and assessments. This observation allows preservice teachers to infer that the edTPA audience values the basic principles of backward design (Wiggins & McTighe, 2005). Additionally, questions in Task 1 and 2 reveal that the edTPA audience values a teacher's knowledge of their students and expects that planning/instruction will build on students' prior learning and other assets. Preservice teachers are therefore able to infer that this audience values constructivist, student-centered pedagogies.

The rubrics provide preservice teachers with additional information, detailing how the edTPA audience will actually interpret written responses. Again, by first analyzing the rubrics for *audience values*, we guide our preservice teachers to ask themselves, "What does my audience consider most important?" which we may assume would represent criteria for a "passing" score. To make these connections clear to our preservice teachers, we ask them to collaboratively complete graphic organizers that connect the commentary language, the rubric language, and what they learn about audience values/beliefs from each (for example, see columns two through four in Figure 11.1).

As we deconstruct the language of the rubrics, we also ask our preservice teachers, "To what extent do these criteria and values represent who you are and what you believe about teaching?" Although many important elements of teaching are not adequately represented in the edTPA questions or rubrics, our candidates most often agree with the core elements represented in the assessment. Finding common ground with their audience may help candidates take greater ownership of their message and feel less intimidated.

Figure 11.1 One Model of Graphic Organizer for Audience Analysis

Task/Question #	Language from prompt	Language from rubric	What audience values	My primary claim	Relevant evidence

Rhetorical Argumentation: Claims, Evidence, Warrants, and Backing

Understanding the audience is just one aspect of advocacy; we also must engage strategies for rhetorical argumentation. We have found the work of Stephen Toulmin (1958/2008) helpful in teaching the relationships between elements of an argument. When working with preservice teachers, we focus on the first four of Toulmin's elements of an argument: claim, grounds, warrant, and backing. The *claim* represents the position being argued for, with the *grounds* involving the reasons and supporting evidence that will support that claim. The *warrant* of an argument is the chain of reasoning that connects the grounds to the claim, building a shared understanding between author and audience. The *backing* then provides support for the reliability or relevance of the warrant in a particular context.

We begin by asking our preservice teachers what claims they want to be able to make about their teaching practices by the end of their student teaching placements. We help them refine their central claims into a clear and overarching statement, such as *I am an effective novice teacher because my planning, instruction, and assessments demonstrate that students are engaged and learning (and when they are not, I have sound ideas about what to do next)*. We ask our preservice teachers, "Is this a claim you hope to confidently make?" and if it is, we ask, "How can you support this claim given what you know of your audience?"

After students consider the overall claim they want to make through their edTPA portfolio, each task provides an opportunity to argue about the efficacy of one element of their teaching. The introduction to Task 1, for example asks candidates to describe the lesson plans they are submitting and explain why their plans are appropriate for their particular students and course content, calling preservice teachers to claim *I plan for instruction in ways that are appropriate for my students and the content I am teaching.* Then, rather than construing each edTPA commentary prompt as a test question, we position these prompts as places to make focused claims about specific elements of their planning, instruction, or assessment practices. For example, within Task 1 they will need to make the claim *I use knowledge about my students to inform my planning decisions*, which they can support using evidence from their planning (e.g., lesson plans, materials, etc.). This layer of analysis also helps preservice teachers notice alignment between the claims they want to make and the evidence they can use to support those claims. To support claims about the effectiveness of their lesson planning decisions, for example, they will need to provide evidence in the form of the actual lesson plans and materials they create.

Helping preservice teachers understand the significance of the warrant can be more challenging but is equally significant. We discuss the significance of connecting claims and evidence in ways that the edTPA evaluators (their audience) will find reasonable, again a valuable skill for advocacy. For this, we ask our preservice teachers to add onto their earlier graphic organizer (see the two rightmost columns in Figure 11.1), helping them keep track of the relationship between their audience values and their own claims and evidence. This work of justifying pedagogical decisions for an external audience— whether it be colleagues, administrators, parents, or policy makers—is an essential form of advocacy that can prepare preservice teachers for future opportunities to advocate for, revise, or reject various types of curricular and/or pedagogical strategies.

Several edTPA prompts also help us introduce the value of *backing,* through which our preservice teachers can practice using theory and research to support the reliability of their claims and reasoning. For example, in Task 2, candidates are asked to suggest changes to their instruction and support the value of these changes supporting these suggestions with examples from research/theory. (Stanford Center for Assessment, 2018, p. 21). We explicitly note that using backing involves authoritatively explaining how our knowledge of the field informs our pedagogical choices, going well beyond merely adding quotes to a term paper. Learning to mobilize backing can help preservice teachers leverage research, reasoning, and data to advocate for themselves and their students.

To help our preservice teachers practice connecting their claims, evidence, warrants, and backing, we also share mentor texts and specific writing strategies. For example, we often use the "3 INs" heuristic for evidence-based writing articulated by Lawrence (2014), which highlights an organizational pattern of *INtroducing* a claim, *INserting* evidence, and then *INterpreting* that evidence in light of the claim. We also encourage students to collaborate with their peers and provide feedback for one another. These writing-specific supports help demystify argument-based writing and provide strategies for teachers to mobilize when they engage in other personal and professional self-advocacy.

Conclusion

Even as we attempt to repurpose the edTPA to teach strategies in audience analysis and rhetorical argumentation, we acknowledge the realities of how this assessment has changed teacher education. The edTPA materials continue to be unnecessarily complex, requiring preservice teachers to move back and forth between explanations, questions, rubrics, and glossaries before they can fully understand what is being asked of them. We each have watched talented student teachers struggle and sometimes fail, then face the emotional, financial, and time burdens involved in retaking portions of the assessment. We have witnessed the challenges that result when student teachers try to engage in instruction that simultaneously suits their students, pleases their cooperating teacher, and satisfies the edTPA requirements. Too often, our first-generation preservice teachers, as well as multilingual preservice teachers for whom English is not their first language, find themselves spending a significant number of extra hours on these tasks. These realities continue to challenge us, pedagogically and ethically.

We also wish the edTPA was the only such challenge our preservice teachers will face. But we know they will go on to districts and schools that may have similar teacher evaluation frameworks, and we know that their own students will be subject to assessments that will attempt to measure and define them. For these reasons, we remain committed to positioning the edTPA as a rhetorical task, in which our preservice teachers can learn to mobilize critical advocacy strategies. They can identify audience values and beliefs, consider the ways these align with or diverge from their own commitments, and use this information to frame their writing. They can analyze the claims their audience expects them to make, consider which evidence their audience will value, and plan ways to use this information to frame what they want to say about their teaching.

With the edTPA, the audience holds considerable power. Administrators, supervisors, colleagues, and policy makers will also hold considerable power and continue to do so across teachers' careers. Even so, we want our student teachers to begin to separate their own professional identities from the opinions of these external audiences. We want them to practice defining themselves. We want them to practice, at this early stage in their careers, the work of articulating what they do and why, which we hope will help empower them to argue for the efficacy of their own pedagogical choices. We hope this work also will prepare them for a time when they are asked to do a time-consuming task, which may be peripheral to their teaching, so that they may strategize to demystify, bound, and repurpose that task in order to pursue their priorities. In short, especially at this early point in their careers, we want our preservice teachers to build strategies for control over their professional identities, voices, and visions.

Suggestions for Teacher Educators

- Engage preservice teachers in a dialogue about the professional assessments used in your location. How can these assessments be mobilized to practice advocating for professional commitments and decisions? What would it look like for candidates to position themselves proactively and professionally in the context of an assessment?

- Engage preservice teachers in analyzing the goals and audiences for professional assessments. What do assessment materials reveal about audience priorities and values? How can preservice teachers practice using this information to frame their responses and to potentially seek out common ground with their audience?

- Invite teacher candidates to make a list of stakeholders in their teaching context. Using an applicable scenario (e.g., selecting new curriculum), role-play how they could explain their position on the issue at hand to the various stakeholders. What claims might they try to make? What evidence might this audience find compelling? How can they explain their reasoning and provide support from research and theory?

- Collaboratively review policy documents or case studies through the lens of rhetorical argumentation. How might an understanding of rhetorical argumentation help deconstruct policy or institutional mandates?

- Identify a controversial issue in ELA (e.g., censored novels or contested approaches to literacy development). After preservice teachers take a well-reasoned stance on the issue, ask them to write a letter to a colleague or administrator who holds a very different opinion.

What We Noticed as We Read This Chapter

Like many of the other contributions in this section, Christine Dawson and Anny Fritzen Case describe the ways they bring everyday advocacy principles into their teacher education contexts. However, they also do the yeoman's work of considering what advocacy can actually mean within the high-stakes contexts of performance evaluation, assessment, and credentialing. Like K–12 teachers' concerns that limited time and institutional standards may constrain their advocacy efforts, the accountability role the edTPA plays in many U.S. teacher education programs is something of a juggernaut that shapes the experiences of myriad new teachers each year. We imagine the substantial requirements of the edTPA may cause some readers to pump the brakes at the idea of diving into advocacy as a component in their courses. Fortunately, Christine and Anny offer some much-needed guidance in this area as they explain how we can approach the high-stakes contexts of edTPA with an advocacy lens. Here are some of the advocacy themes we noticed as we read:

- *Framing and reframing are primary first steps toward advocacy.* As they describe the work they do *within* the constraints of edTPA assessments, Christine and Anny also express this experience as the first of "many moments when our preservice teachers will be called to showcase their professional decisions." They help their preservice teachers shift the frame of edTPA from a external standardized assessment that defines their abilities as teachers to a reframe of the experience "as an argument, which preservice teachers must make to advocate for their advancement and choices." We can't overestimate the value of the reframe, particularly in this case. When teachers see themselves as in control of the argument (and the narrative as we have referred to it throughout this book), they begin "to find and raise their voices even when addressing a powerful audience." Starting with the edTPA, a mandatory part of their preservice experience, strikes us as a brilliant choice.

Questions to consider: Are there particular kinds of testing endemic to your own teaching context? How might you view those tests through an advocacy lens? How might you help your preservice teachers do so?

- *Framing and reframing are connected to "reading" an audience.* As Christine and Anny explain, "Different audiences value and prioritize different things, so 'reading' an audience can empower teachers to target their message more deliberately and proactively—a critical component of effective advocacy." We couldn't agree more. The way we target a message to a parent audience is different from the way we target the same message to an administrator or an assessor. We're reminded of a moment when Cathy was coteaching an 11th grade English class in which students were preparing for a standardized test essay that asked them to write a letter to their principal about a dress code issue. When she asked them to consider the audience, they (quite naturally) responded the audience was the principal; when she suggested that the principal would never actually read the letter, they came to understand that the test assessor was the actual audience. When the coteachers pushed the students to further consider who the assessor might be and what they might bring to the reading of the students' essays, the students suggested the readers might be teachers who would spend 20 to 30 minutes reading each essay. When the coteachers burst that bubble by telling them that readers for this test were required to have completed 2 years of college and that they spent about 2 minutes reading each essay, a light bulb went off in the students' minds about how they might construct an essay that would fit that rhetorical situation.

Questions to consider: How might you introduce to your own students the concept of audience with respect to testing? How might this emergent understanding impact their approach to testing and to advocacy in testing.

- *Advocacy is a part of teacher identity.* Christine and Anny's response to the edTPA—to meet it with advocacy—is not simply a method for navigating the hurdles of the teaching profession, it also emphasizes advocacy as a core part of teacher identity: "We want [our preservice teachers] to practice defining themselves. We want them to practice, at this early stage in their careers, the work of articulating what they do and why, which we hope will help empower them to argue for the efficacy of their own pedagogical choices."

  Questions to consider: How might you create situations in which your students can practice this work of "articulating what they do and why"? What audiences might they target? What issues might they target?

Finally, even if you are in a schooling context that does not engage with the edTPA, the paradigm of accountability around teacher education isn't going away anytime soon. We encourage *all* readers—teachers and teacher educators—to look at the savvy approaches to working advocacy into the very foundations of accountability systems. This chapter highlights advocacy as something that does not simply happen alongside the bigger stuff but that can integrally inform how teachers see their roles in classrooms, as an important contribution to the teacher advocacy conversation. The moxie that Christine and Anny demonstrate here should serve as inspiration for teachers across settings.

References

Lawrence, A. M. (2014). Three heuristics for writing and revising qualitative research articles in English education. *Teaching/Writing: The Journal of Writing Teacher Education, 3*(2), 98–122.

Stanford Center for Assessment, Learning, and Equity. (2018). *Secondary English language arts assessment handbook.* Stanford, CA: Board of Trustees of the Leland Stanford Junior University.

Toulmin, S. E. (1958/2008). *The uses of argument* (Updated ed.). New York: Cambridge University Press.

Wiggins, G., & McTighe, J. (2005) *Understanding by design* (2nd ed.). Alexandria, VA: Association for Supervision and Curriculum Development ASCD.

Chapter 12

Writing Into Identity and Action

Advocacy Through Authorship

Sarah Hochstetler

Sarah Hochstetler is a former secondary English teacher, NWP fellow, and current Professor of English education at Illinois State University where she teaches in the English Teacher Education program and other pedagogy-focused courses in the department of English. In this chapter, she shares a particular assignment she uses with preservice teachers to connect writing and advocacy.

Like many first-year teachers, I spent my early high school English teacher months settling into my classroom and figuring out my identity in a new but not unfamiliar space. A small but growing part of that critical identity development was finding a way of situating myself as an everyday advocate, as someone who could leverage my expertise to create the changes that I knew mattered most. I navigated the day-to-day instructional and curricular demands of teaching while also working to make sense of how those demands intersected with my responsibilities to my students, my community, and the profession-at-large to speak up for literacy learning. With the aid of a few specific resources—namely, invitations to write and support to publish that writing—I was able to realize a version of myself as an advocate that felt true and that advanced over time to become central to my professional sense of self.

In my current role as a writing-teacher educator, I proactively embed into the required methods courses I teach experiences that mirror the invitations and support I received as a novice teacher. In this way I work to foster in my students an identity grounded in everyday advocacy. I draw on scholarship in socially just teaching and critical literacies, as well as my early experiences as a beginning teacher, to build opportunities for my students to define, discuss, and practice advocacy through authorship (Boyd, 2017; Gorlewski, 2018; Hochstetler, 2011; Moje, 2007; Paris & Alim, 2017). One of my aims in integrating advocacy-oriented thinking and writing into my methods course-work is to normalize advocacy in preservice teachers' framing of their professional selves and help them publicly assert their expertise to, among other things, change the narrative around education through publication, which I define as sharing their insight and ideas about literacy in public ways. More concretely, I aspire to expand my students' conceptions of what it means to be a high school English teacher to include writer *and* advocate (in addition to content area specialist and pedagogical expert) for the purposes of effecting change. These efforts work toward answering the field's call to encourage preservice teachers to become agents of political and social change (Alsup et al., 2006).

In this chapter I highlight one assignment, the *Inquiry Project* (*IP*), from my capstone writing methods course for preservice English Teacher Education students, designed as a potential pathway for cultivating and sustaining advocate identities with action. I begin by describing this assignment and how it asks students to practice advocacy through authorship in one public space; I explain how students struggle with taking on the agency required of the assignment and the ways I use the Everyday Advocacy website to mitigate their fears and concerns; I articulate possible views on success and effectiveness for the *IP* assignment; and I conclude with a continued call for teacher educators to more purposely embed invitations to advocacy in their mentoring of pre-service teachers and teacher candidates to better position them to enact and sustain advocacy as part of their multifaceted identities as secondary English teachers.

The *Inquiry Project* Assignment

Project Overview and Evolution

The *Inquiry Project* has been a mainstay of my writing methods courses since I started working alongside preservice secondary ELA teachers. Though its format, intended audience, and proposed mediums and publication forums have evolved over the years, what has remained constant is its focus on writing for advocacy. This assignment invites writing methods students into the discourse of the profession by asking them to: 1) compose an argument around an issue related to teaching secondary writers and writing, and, 2) contribute to ongoing conversations in that area. For example, a student might reframe a common problem and offer potentially innovative solutions to the problem from their perspective as a new educator.

Students have written their *IPs* for an audience of themselves and their peers in our methods sequence, and that audience has expanded to include readers like practicing teachers via our state NCTE affiliate publication. Students have written more recently for *Teachers, Profs, Parents: Writers Who Care*, a peer reviewed blog about "writing, the teaching of writing, and the power of engaging young writers in craft and story" for teachers, teacher educators, and community members (writerswhocare.wordpress.com/about/). The present iteration of the *IP* asks students to compose a submission appropriate for the *From Campus to Classroom* column in NCTE's *English Journal*. This column, new to the journal in 2018, "seeks to share the viewpoints of those poised to enter the classroom" and positions the insights of preservice teachers as having the "power to provoke veteran teachers and teacher educators to think differently [by] revisiting familiar assignments, reconsidering current perspectives, and reexamining long-held beliefs about teaching and learning" (*English Journal*). The similarities between the goals of the *IP* and the column's purpose are clear, and both the project and outlet support my commitment to authentic writing, in this case for students' writing for an audience beyond me, their professor—thus my capitalizing on the strong match for my students' forays into public writing for advocacy.

Points of Tension: The Interplay of Advocacy and Identity

It's not difficult for my students to start this project. They know what they're curious about as it relates to teaching writing and writers, especially as they investigate their clinical sites through equity audits and learn about their own students through writing workshops and regular conferring. They are adept at identifying, articulating, and researching a problem, formulating an argument, and supporting it with evidence from reliable sources through writing appropriate for various audiences. While the pragmatic part of this project is writing about writing and the young writers they've built relationships with, a significant piece of the project is self-interrogation. In asking students to develop a potential contribution to ongoing conversations that challenges accepted truths and practices, this assignment asks *Where does advocacy figure into your thinking about yourself as a teacher of writers*? The real challenge to this assignment manifests in whether my students feel they have the authority to advocate, which often includes pushing back against the status quo. Further, the assignment invites them to reveal their ideas in a public space, requiring them to claim an agentic stance. So, even those who already self-identify as writers and advocates may still struggle with the part of the *Inquiry Project* that requires students to "put themselves out there." Regardless of the publishing end-point of their writing, the product is still "out there" and shared among peers and mentors, and it still requires them to take steps toward entering larger professional dialogue through agitating for some kind of change.

The most demanding aspects of this project center on the interplay of advocacy and identity. At its core, the *IP* presses itself on preservice teachers' identities and the extent to which they see their ideas as valuable and their voices as carrying weight in a public venue. For me, this is another opportunity and entry point to in-class discussions about everyday advocacy and teacher identity. Much like how my students and I talk about ways to coach their future secondary students in being and in becoming writers beyond the scope of a semester, my preservice teachers engage in a parallel uncovering of how they can coach each other in being and in becoming advocates beyond our classroom. Again, though some of my preservice students already self-identify as writers and advocates, braiding these together for the purposes of joining an ongoing dialogue about challenging problematic aspects of teaching and learning creates a generative pressure point in their emerging understandings of who they want to be as responsive literacy educators.

Everyday Advocacy as Heuristic

As indicated above, students' drafting of the *Inquiry Project* tends to slow around their public writing, the most agentic piece of their project. It becomes clear, as we workshop these pieces, that many students are intimidated by how to connect their developing beliefs around, for example, advocating for instructional strategies that align in socially just ways of teaching writing with considerations for the audience and proposed forum. They have ideas for advocacy but fear they aren't "good enough" to share, especially when their audience is more public than our classroom.

A New Vision

Recently, I began to introduce excerpts from the Everyday Advocacy website to guide students' thinking toward advocacy and authorship and mitigate some of their concerns. I couch our initial conversations in the Everyday Advocacy site's language of "a new vision for teacher professionalism" (Everyday Advocacy, n.d.a). In the context of the *IP*, this language is generative in reframing for my students their novice positions as positions of agency and power. Part of this process includes us sitting with and analyzing discomfort to give shape to the meaning of advocacy in our context. Common questions from class dialogue include: *What does it mean to be an advocate? Who among us are advocates? What role does privilege play in our levels of commitment to advocacy? What could it look like to advocate from the position of (preservice) teacher? How does one get to claim authority? Is there a particular measure of success in advocacy for (preservice) teachers? What is at risk if we don't take up or sustain advocacy as an essential core of our identities?* We move through versions of these questions toward *How can we support our growing advocacy stances or address feelings of inadequacy that might dissuade us from taking up advocacy?* It is in these spaces of wondering that I am able to circle back to discussions about what it means to be an agent of change and link it with our professional responsibilities to raise our voices to defend or support or reframe public understanding around literacy teaching.

Three Core Ideas

Another essential tool from the Everyday Advocacy website that I use in addressing my preservice teachers, who are learning about and navigating advocacy in the context of the *Inquiry Project*, is "three core ideas" (Everyday Advocacy, n.d.b). Students are heartened when I share this framework and explain how the core ideas move in tandem with the typical organization of the *Inquiry Project*: Describe your experiences or how you came to the topic/problem (#1: storytelling). Situate the topic/problem (#2: identifying and framing). And propose a new take/solution (#3: taking action). The core ideas provide shape for making an advocacy-centered argument in a piece of writing.

Sustainability

Finally, the everyday advocacy approach suggests sustainability, which undergirds my teaching into and through the *Inquiry Project*. More specifically, the site posts several mentor texts from practicing teachers for preservice teachers to consider as they give shape to their own advocacy. The message is: advocacy is an ongoing part of one's daily practice. What I appreciate most about this assumption, which is threaded throughout the Everyday Advocacy site, is that it forwards the expectation of (and provides a community of support for) an advocate identity. Leveraging one's expertise to affect change through writing is not a one-time project of informing others: it is *the* project of being a literacy educator.

Effective *Inquiry Projects*

My general measure of an effective *IP* is based on how well students are able to address the rhetorical situation of the invitation to write and to demonstrate both their thoughtful consideration of what it means to be an advocate and how advocacy can be realized through authorship in a public way. At this stage in their professional development I believe it is most important for students to imagine ways their own writing can be a tool for advocacy and to recognize the available formats of writing and locations for publication (e.g., blog posts written for neighbors and friends, open letters in the local paper, prepared statements read at school board meetings, presentations at conferences, etc.) that can move their ideas about literacy education and advocacy into the open. In the case of writing for *From Campus to Classroom* or similar submission-based publication outlets, I make clear that acceptance for publication is not a marker of success. Their writing is still published informally and reaches an audience of peers and faculty in our program, and they are still complicating their thinking about advocacy.

Some students have been able to publish their writing in more formal ways. Last year, a group of students from one section of writing methods submitted their *IPs* in the form of a panel at a regional teaching conference. The title of their session was *Putting the Myth of Teacher Neutrality to Rest: Culturally Relevant Pedagogy and Student Writer Voice*. The following semester, Kaitlyn Remian, a student from my course, submitted her *IP* to the *From Campus to Classroom* column in *English Journal*, and it has since been published (Remian, 2019).

The outcomes of the *Inquiry Project* assignment have been effective because many preservice teachers come away from it with confirmation that their emerging professional perspectives and contributions do matter, can be elevated to informal or formal public spaces for authentic audiences, and are critical to an advocate identity.

Final Thoughts

The stakes are high for educators as we collectively navigate systems of reform and resist narratives that incorrectly frame literacy teaching and learning. I argue that educators at all levels, from preservice to practicing, have a responsibility to engage publicly by contributing to conversations about literacy education from a critical perspective. As a writing methods instructor, I work with preservice teachers with different understandings of advocacy and different views on how it pertains to their developing identities as secondary ELA teachers. I hold up the *Inquiry Project* assignment as one way to begin or extend the thinking and practices of novice professionals as they consider what it means to author advocacy. While some students already conceive of themselves as writers and/or advocates, a project like this invites all students to situate themselves as experts and advocates in public spaces as an essential part of their multiple teacher identities, which is necessary for an agentic stance and persistence in the profession.

What We Noticed as We Read This Chapter

Zooming in on a singular assignment within her teacher education courses, Sarah Hochstetler's chapter connects the instructional goals of her *Inquiry Project* with her own day-to-day lesson plans and pedagogy. Sarah doesn't simply share the assignment with us, she takes us into her classroom contexts so that we can see the reasons she takes up this project the way that she does. While we think this is particularly valuable for readers who might adopt a similar project within their own teacher education courses, we also think that this metacognitive approach to instruction related to advocacy offers a powerful guide around lesson design for future teachers as well. By allowing readers to follow along with how this instructional unit unfolds, Sarah's chapter makes a powerful companion text to the assignment itself; we can imagine teachers utilizing the *Inquiry Project* assignment *and* having students read and discuss Sarah's chapter to better understand how her personal goals shape her instructional decisions. In Sarah's approach, we noticed the following elements, which might help other English educators integrate advocacy into their teaching:

- *Identifying as an advocate yourself helps students identify as advocates.* In describing the aims of this assignment, Sarah offers a powerful description of how an advocacy-focused identity shaped her identity as a teacher and researcher: "With the aid of a few specific resources . . . I was able to realize a version of myself as an advocate that felt true and that advanced over time to become central to my professional sense of self." As Sarah digs into the work that is the *Inquiry Project* instructional design, she offers a clear vision of advocacy as a dialogic process. Her model—one that shifts teacher identities through reflection—is a powerful one, that echoes the intent of the *Writers Who Care* blog as a space for authentic engagement (as Leah Zuidema describes in Chapter 13).

Questions to consider: As you think about your own history as a teacher and a citizen, what experiences with advocacy have you had? How might those experiences help you identify as an advocate and also help the preservice teachers with whom you work to identify as advocates?

- *Going public with advocacy can take many forms.* As Sarah explains, while advocacy is indeed a public undertaking, it's also a scaffolded process. Some students, as they develop their advocacy identities, may not yet feel comfortable communicating their newfound understandings outside the safety of their own classroom communities. And that's fine. Ultimately, the personal nature of Sarah's *Inquiry Project* is about allowing students to feel confident when they confront power structures and to feel ready to "push back against the status quo." For Sarah, this is a process of "self-interrogation," and it is a process of renewal that, we think, educators must engage in continually throughout their careers.

Questions to consider: What publics can you imagine preservice teachers writing for? How might you scaffold that experience for them?

We see in Sarah's description of the *Inquiry Project* a layered approach to endowing students with a sense of confidence, splashing away the flotsam of uncertainty when students wonder if they are "good enough" for the work they must take up.

References

Alsup, J., Emig, J., Pradl, G., Tremmel, R., Yagelski, R. P., Alvine, L., DeBlase, G., Petrone, R., Sawyer, M. (2006). The state of English education and a vision for its future: A call to arms. *English Education, 38*(4), 278–294.

Boyd, A. S. (2017). *Social justice literacies in the English classroom: Teaching practice in action.* New York, NY: Teachers College Press.

National Council of Teachers of English. (2019). Columns and Column Editors. *English Journal.* Retrieved from http://www2.ncte.org/resources/journals/english-journal/columns-and-editors/

Everyday Advocacy. (n.d.a). Retrieved from https://everydayadvocacy.org/a-new-vision-of-teacher-professionalism/

Everyday Advocacy. (n.d.b). *Learn: Three Core Ideas.* Retrieved from https://everydayadvocacy.org/three-core-ideas/

Gorlewski, J. (2018). *English language arts: A critical introduction.* New York, NY: Routledge.

Hochstetler, S. (2011). From consuming to producing: The potential of preservice teacher scholarship in English teacher preparation. *Language Arts Journal of Michigan, 27*(1), 43–46. doi:10.9707/2168-149X.1835

Moje, E. (2007). Developing socially just subject-matter instruction: A review of the literature on disciplinary literacy teaching. *Review of Research in Education, 31,* 1–44. https://doi.org/10.3102/0091732X07300046001

Paris, J., & Alim, H. L. (2017). *Culturally sustaining pedagogies: Teaching and learning for justice in a changing world.* New York, NY: Teachers College Press.

Remian, K. (2019). Building bridges for English language learners through multimodal writing. *English Journal, 108*(6), 99–96.

Chapter 13

Sustainable Advocacy

Blogging to Effect Change

Leah A. Zuidema

Leah Zuidema is a former high school teacher and English education professor. She is now Vice President for Online & Graduate Education at Dordt University and former president of the National Council of Teachers of English. In this chapter she introduces us to a project she cofounded, the Writers Who Care blog. She invites us to consider how public writing becomes advocacy.

As educators, we often seem to run directly against the wind of popular opinion about what should happen in our classrooms. In our communities and social media feeds, we are surrounded by friends, family members, and coworkers who spent years as students in schools—and who assume that they know what education should be like. Consequently, when we want our students to try new things, our expertise is undervalued, and we often have to make a case to gain administrative support, to garner cooperation from colleagues, and to help parents, community members, and news and social media contacts understand the value of what we are doing.

In other words, we need ongoing advocacy for what we as educators know is best for students. But the thought of taking on regular advocacy in the midst of everything else that we do raises hard questions: *How can we fit advocacy into our weekly rhythms inside and outside the classroom? Where do we find time to do this? Can we advocate in an energizing way that gives us joy rather than a piling-on-a-dreaded-task way that depletes us?*

These are some of the important questions that you are likely asking, and they are the same questions that I and other cofounders of the *Writers Who Care* (*WWC*) blog (https://writerswhocare.wordpress.com/) asked as we grappled with how to advocate for something that mattered a great deal to us. This chapter explains what motivated us to engage in ongoing advocacy, why we designed *WWC* as a multiauthor edited blog, and how our project has worked out.

We Had to Do Something

We didn't set out to write a blog. We weren't planning to become everyday advocates. We were a group of hot, tired, and frustrated educators who felt that we couldn't take it anymore. We had to do something. It was July 2013, at the convention for what is now known as ELATE (English Language Arts Teacher Educators), part of the National Council of Teachers of English. The dry Colorado sunshine was spiking the temperature in the room where about a dozen of us from the Commission on Writing Teacher Education were in working meetings. Over a few days, we kept circling back to the same problem: we saw an urgent need for students across grade levels to engage in authentic writing, but we also saw the many barriers that teachers faced when they tried to implement curriculum, instruction, and assessment for authentic writing. We were commiserating, venting, and looking for ways to change the narratives surrounding the classrooms and schools where we and our teacher colleagues were trying to teach the kinds of writing that we knew would be beneficial for students.

We had a common cause, and we were motivated. But what could we do to try to change public opinion? How could we make a difference in our schools and communities? Naturally, as writing teachers, we saw writing as a potential solution—but we also knew that as with any writing challenge, we would need to work through questions about genre, audience, purpose, and situation (GAPS).

Designing for Sustainable Advocacy

Through our conversations about audience and purpose, we soon realized that we had another problem. Most of us in the room were college and university professors, and when we wrote about education, it was usually for other professors and researchers.

We wrote the kinds of things that most of our neighbors would never read or want to read and only our most devoted friends and family members would show any interest in. If we wanted to change others' opinions in a localized way—in our neighborhood schools and communities—we couldn't write research articles, theoretical essays, and books. We needed to write in genres that would spark interest in readers outside the academia community, and we needed to share our writing in venues that would reach the readers we hoped to influence.

Soon we arrived at the idea of blogging. We liked the possibility of shorter, easy-to-read pieces that would spotlight classroom stories and successes. Blog posts could also include links that would support interested readers in digging deeper into research articles and teaching texts. We were excited about the potential for sharing posts through social media, noting that this might help us to be proactive in changing stories about school writing while also allowing us to quickly respond when we wanted to counter troubling ideas and narratives. We liked the potential of a blog to keep promoting our ideas across time, continually and cumulatively adding bursts of new content to public conversations about writing education.

However, it was the idea of regular writing that also gave us pause. Should one of us be designated as "the blogger" while others took on other advocacy projects? This idea was quickly dismissed. None of us had the time or energy to maintain a regular blog. We wondered how long it would take for any one person to run out of new things to say and what problems might result if one person were to "speak for" the commission we were representing. We realized, too, that to be effective, the blogger might have to share stories and ideas that could be interpreted as challenging to their school or seen as going against the grain of their community's norms, and we wanted to avoid putting one person in a spotlight that might start to shine with an uncomfortably bright glare.

It was at this point in our meeting that we started to seriously discuss the concept that we eventually chose and that has been in effect since that meeting in 2013: the edited multiauthor blog.

Advocacy Collaborations and Invitations

As we recognized the limitations of an individually authored blog, we deliberated about the pros and cons of having a small team of bloggers who would rotate through the author role. However, as we considered trying a team-authored blog, we realized that we could create greater opportunities—and more sustainable advocacy—if instead we were to have a team of contributing editors who would also invite posts from a much bigger cadre of guest authors. Rather than generating all of the content, the editorial team would maintain the vision for the blog and ensure that posts fulfilled our desired purpose (to promote authentic writing instruction) while matching with the interests and needs of our audience—our friends and neighbors across the United States.

This was the model for *WWC* when we began the blog in 2013, and the blog continues to operate today as a multiauthor edited publication. The remainder of this short chapter explains more about how we see this kind of blog as a way of creating sustainable advocacy.[*]

Through a design decision that has increased the longevity and impact of the *WWC* blog, classroom teachers, preservice teachers, and parents have authored many entries, making "authentic writing" more vibrant and meaningful through stories about the writers and about writing in their classrooms and homes. For example, during her student teaching semester as a university senior, Iris Treinies and her professor, Tracey Flores, coauthored a post about their El Puente partnership with adult literacy learners in their community (Flores & Treinies, 2019). There is great value in having the voice of a preservice teacher on the blog, as it shows in a compelling way that authentic writing instruction is important (and attainable) at all stages in a teacher's career—and that it is something that is learned over time. Preservice and early-career teachers provide valuable perspective when they help parents, other teachers, administrators, and professors to see the classroom as they encounter it.

Likewise, pieces from parents also have great value in the shared advocacy space of a multiauthor, edited blog. Among the most powerful *WWC* entries is "Writing Delaney," in which Jonathan Bush shares his reflections on writing an obituary upon the death of his daughter. In a piece that was widely shared across social media as soon as it was published (Bush, 2018), he weaves together his memories of Delaney with his observations of the role of writing in grief and in healing. Parent-authored pieces on lighter topics also have relevance and impact, as is readily evident in "My Kid is Creating YouTube Videos?"—a piece by Jonathan Rochelle that also experienced broad readership (2014). These authors and the many others who contribute to *Teachers, Profs, Parents: Writers*

---

[*] Readers seeking more information about the rhetorical decisions and design choices that we made as editors can read about the development and impact of *WWC* in Hochstetler, Letcher, Jeffers, Warrington, & Buescher, 2016 and Zuidema, Hochstetler, Letcher, & Turner, 2014.

Who Care make a compelling case for authentic writing instruction, personalizing the issue and illustrating that it matters far beyond the walls of a university.

Creating Energy and Impact

One of the great advantages of the multiauthor, edited model for *WWC* is that no one person "owns" the blog. In fact, the four of us who were founding editors (Kristen Hawley Turner, Mark Letcher, Sarah Hochstetler, and myself) eventually imposed term limits on ourselves and after a few years rotated out of our editorial roles, one by one. Yet the blog continues under the guidance of new editors and with the support of numerous peer reviewers. Every two weeks, there is another *WWC* post that illustrates and emphasizes the importance of authentic writing instruction. *Writers Who Care* maintains an ongoing open call for manuscripts, and the blog continues to be a place where any teacher, professor, or parent with a compelling insight about authentic writing instruction can share their ideas with the world.

Creating an editorial team proved to be important in more ways than we anticipated. The collaboration that was required for our editorial work also energized us. Out of necessity, we regularly talked with one another about authentic writing in video call meetings, and as we coached authors to shape their manuscripts for the blog, we grew more skilled at describing relevant teaching/learning practices and more fluent in sharing the research and theoretical frameworks that grounded our work. We had regular opportunities to speak, write, listen, and read in connection with our passion for authentic writing.

That energy spread to our contributing authors, and—as the blog matured—to our peer reviewers, too. We were all encouraging one another as we shared and responded to important stories from our authors. It was especially exciting when a post got a high number of shares and reads, or when we heard from someone in our *WWC* community about how a post had made a difference in their school or classroom. We found that our networks grew, and, perhaps best of all, we developed friendships through our shared interests and efforts. These somewhat unexpected benefits further energized our advocacy and increased the value of the time that we invested together.

As this chapter goes to press, the 7th anniversary of *Writers Who Care* is approaching. I can confidently say that the blog has lasted longer, reached more readers, and empowered more advocates to make their stories known than if any one of us had tried blogging alone or even if our small team had simply shared the author's chair. By agreeing to share and distribute our everyday efforts, we created a sustainable approach to advocacy.

Author's Note: I am grateful for the collaboration of the founding editorial team for Writers Who Care, for the thoughtful and skillful work that continues to be done by those who have since taken the lead for WWC (as listed at https://writerswhocare .wordpress.com/authors/), and for the National Council of Teachers of English, which brought us together and has frequently highlighted posts from WWC in through the NCTE Inbox newsletter.

What We Noticed as We Read This Chapter

Before diving into what makes Leah Zuidema's chapter so compelling, we should note that we have been fans and readers of *Writers Who Care* for several years. It is this appreciation of the work that Leah and her colleagues engaged in that has led us both to contribute articles to the blog and to seek out Leah's thoughts for this book. In reflecting on the journey toward cocreating *Writers Who Care*, Leah notes several themes that get to the heart of advocacy.

- *Making time for and finding joy in advocacy work.* In questioning how to do the work of advocacy on top of the many, *many* other commitments that tax teachers' time, Leah asks, "Can we advocate in an energizing way that gives us joy rather than a piling-on-a-dreaded-task way that depletes us?" This joyous feeling is one that we—as teachers and as teacher educators— should consider more than we do. Advocacy, as often represented in popular media as well as in some of the chapters in this volume, is seen as something that takes a toll on advocates. We expend energy, materials, and time toward advocacy efforts. The gains of advocacy are too seldom considered or valued. This transactive nature of the work, described in this volume, often occludes the personal, professional, and moral pay off of working toward just literacy practices and possibilities. Leah's chapter is a call for all to see advocacy work as energizing or—depending on where you may be in your career—*re*energizing rather than as one more chore.

Questions to consider: When reading Leah's chapter, were there particular moments in her story that elicited joy? Instead of looking at your advocacy as a kind of charity to help *others*, can you explicitly name ways your efforts would cause *you* joy?

- *Writing is a purposeful tool within advocacy efforts. Writers Who Care* is a platform on which advocacy can take place and also a form of advocacy in and of itself. It asks you to consider how you communicate about issues that are meaningful for you and the ways writing—as a tool for persuasion, as a means of organization, as a means of presenting data, etc.—shapes what you are doing and with whom. For Leah and her colleagues, we can see how blogging functions as a sustainable platform. For you, the medium might be something different. It is important to recognize that the efforts that Leah recounts are specifc to the genre of writing they selected. As a blog conveys "shorter, easy-to-read" articles, part of her group's advocacy efforts required participants to write within that specific genre

Questions to consider: As instructors of writing—and likely as passionate writers ourselves, if only we had the time!—how do the styles and modalities of composition shape your advocacy efforts? What kinds of writing and platforms for writing might best fit your advocacy and that of the teachers with whom you work?

- *Shared leadership matters in advocacy.* The possibility of distributing leadership for *Writers Who Care*, as well as for quickly and publicly amplifying the teacher voices on the blog, underscored their design decisions for the publishing platform. But Leah also points to the need for finding sustainable models for advocacy work. As Leah shares, no one person has time to do everything; finding collaborators and allies in this work allows us to sustain the energy it demands. We also notice how Leah and her team wisely developed new editors over time; too often, advocacy efforts that rely on particular leaders fail when those leaders move onto other projects. Focusing on the effort, rather than the leader, is one way to keep the work sustainable.

Questions to consider: As you think about your own advocacy work, who might you bring in as allies and partners? What issues of concern do you share? How might you work together to create a sustainable project?

- *How we write matters in terms of whom we will reach.* As Leah explains, as university professors, the *Writers Who Care Team* was accustomed to writing in a particular way: "Most of us in the room were college and university professors, and when we wrote about education, it was usually for other professors and researchers. We wrote the kinds of things that most of our neighbors would never read or want to read and only our most devoted friends and family members would show any interest in." When we try to reach out to other audiences for our advocacy, the way we write needs to shift. The multiple audiences for blog posts—particularly as articles are written for teachers as well as parents—helps emphasize the different linguistic and rhetorical choices we must make as effective and inviting advocates.

Questions to consider: What changes might you need to make in your writing to reach audiences that are new to you? (The *Writers Who Care* site offers resources to help, including a Tips for Writing for Parents sheet.) How might you invite your students to think about linguistic and rhetorical shifts in their writing?

Leah's chapter functions as an invitation. We invite you to read it as you explore the *Writers Who Care* site. Use this site to reflect on what inspires you—both the content and the platform as possible models. The site is an open-access journal to which you and your fellow teachers and preservice teachers might consider submitting your work.

References

Bush, J. (2018, December 10). Writing Delaney: Composing in the aftermath of life and loss. Retrieved from *Teachers, Profs, Parents: Writers Who Care* website: https:// writerswhocare.wordpress.com/2018/12/10/writing-delaney-composing-in-the -aftermath-of-life-and-loss/

Flores, T. T., & Treinies, I. (2019, April 8). El Puente: Building bridges through lan-guage and literacy partnerships. Retrieved from *Teachers, Profs, Parents: Writers Who Care* website: https://writerswhocare.wordpress.com/2019/04/08/el-puente-building -bridges-through-language-and-literacy-partnerships/

Hochstetler, S., Letcher, M., Jeffers, L., Warrington, A., & Buescher, E. (2016). "The big-gest surprise was the feeling of empowerment": Teachers sharing stories for advocacy and transformation. *Voices from the Middle, 24*(1), 44–47.

Rochelle, J. (2014, October 20). My kid is creating YouTube videos? Retrieved from *Teachers, Profs, Parents: Writers Who Care* website: https://writerswhocare.wordpress .com/2014/10/20/my-kid-is-creating-youtube-videos/

Zuidema, L. A., Hochstetler, S., Letcher, M., & Turner, K. H. (2014). Writers who care: Advocacy blogging as teachers - professors - parents. *Teaching/Writing: The Journal of Writing Teacher Education, 3,* 81–89.

Chapter 14

After the Walkout

Everyday Advocacy Meets Political Advocacy

Robin Fuxa

Robin Fuxa is a professor at Oklahoma State University in the College of Education and Human Sciences. As she explains in this chapter, her commitments to advocacy run deep. The recent teacher walkout in Oklahoma led her to introduce multiple kinds of advocacy to her students. By focusing on how literacy efforts are tied to the broader labor movements that have shifted the teaching profession over the years, her narrative explores how her preservice teachers' enthusiasm for "big A" advocacy mirrors powerful lessons about growth, about education, and about our role as allies alongside larger movements.

Let me start this story with a little background about the much-heralded teacher walkout in the state of Oklahoma that began on April 2, 2018. For over a decade prior to the walkout, Oklahoma had begun to garner national attention for the dearth of resources our public school teachers were facing. Some educators looked back, remembering the successful Oklahoma walkout in 1990 that culminated in the passage of House Bill 1017, celebrated by educators and parent advocates for its much needed raise in teacher pay (Oklahoma had been forty-ninth in pay at the time) and limits on class size. A mere two years after the passage of HB 1017, supported by those who felt the price tag for it was too high, State Question 640 was voted into law. The passing of this measure means a three-quarters majority approval of both chambers of the Oklahoma legislature is now required to pass *any* revenue raising bill. After the economy crashed in 2008, with SQ 640 so badly hindering the potential to raise revenue, the legislature began waiving the limits on class size that teachers had won.

Until the threat of the recent walkout loomed, leading up to the 2018 legislative session, there had not been a *single* tax increase for any reason successfully ushered through the state legislature. Not surprisingly, Oklahoma led the nation in the deepest cuts, by far, to the per pupil funds allotted for public schools when adjusted for inflation, hovering at 28.2% from fiscal year 2008 to 2018. Yes, funds for public schools were scarce in many states across the nation, but Oklahoma school funding was too often and too easily compared to lack of rain at the peak of the Dust Bowl—and this drought resulted in an exodus of certified teachers. Many north Texas districts pay far above their state minimum salary, and I would be rather surprised if the migration of Oklahoma teachers across the Red River to Texas wasn't visible from space at one point. At least it seemed so; recent and not-so-recent grads' reference requests for jobs in surrounding states flooded my inbox.

Coincidentally, not long before the walkout began, I had worked with a small team of undergraduate and graduate students to form the student Education Advocacy Organization at Oklahoma State University where I serve as Director of Professional Education, the office that oversees certification and accreditation for the educator prep programs across the institution. Just as the preservice teachers and in-service teachers in the Advocacy Organization really got rolling in earnest, the 2018 walkout kicked off with a kind of frenzied energy, feeding high hopes for many Oklahoma teachers for the first time in a long time. The group was just beginning the process to apply for official university organization status—but it immediately became clear that work on the details of our student organization constitution would have to wait while we focused on the looming strike.

The members of the group—preservice teachers, in-service teachers, and university faculty—jumped into advocacy. They had set up a GroupMe chat via text message, and they updated one another with information from the capitol and about our upcoming meetings. Some faculty held their classes at the capitol, about one hour southwest of our main campus, for those who could make it and offered an optional assignment for those who could not. Others charged forward on campus, holding critical conversations in class. Our undergraduate preservice teachers and graduate students who were already teaching were all eager for a space to channel their concerns. They shared their photos of the walkout with one another as well as their letters to policy makers. They reported their face-to-face conversations with legislators, often noting, "They're really not that scary." And they quickly learned that some policy makers who were not allies would try to steer the conversation away from the issues of pay and resources, which enabled our students to offer sound advice to others: "Don't let them tell you what else they've done for the state; keep the conversation focused on why you're there—public school funding." They reminded one another where to track legislative bills and how; they watched the news daily for updates and stayed up-to-date with Oklahoma Policy Institute reports, a key non-partisan think tank for those seeking up-to-date information. They (along with countless other educators, parents, and allies) took careful note not only of legislators' voting records leading up to and during the walkout, but also of those who treated teachers dismissively or, worse, demonized them for finally standing up for their students. (As an aside, I take a great deal of comfort now in the fact that few of the latter are still in office, having not made it past their June 2018 primaries in most cases.)

The walkout came to an abrupt and unsatisfactory ending as its ninth day closed, and teachers returned to school with little more than the raise that was initially offered just days before the walkout began in an unsuccessful effort to *prevent* its occurrence. At this point, the school year was nearly a wrap as well, and we debriefed to the best of our ability, all of us rather emotionally spent and with a mix of sadness and anger. The members of the Education Advocacy Organization talked about how successfully the group had updated one another during the walkout—a team effort that involved piecing together the latest revenue options being proposed and the opposition each was facing and why. But the experienced teachers in the group also noted that fewer of the preservice teachers had ventured *inside* the capitol building. Most stayed outside in the comfort of the crowd with their signs, with a couple of notable exceptions. Those few teacher candidates who met with legislators often did so in the company of at least one educator parent who was also very involved in advocacy. I don't minimize anyone's important step in their advocacy journeys: it is certainly commendable to join the fight at the capitol in any capacity. However, this realization led the student officer team and me to begin discussing ways we could expand opportunities by increasing our members' comfort level with face-to-face advocacy work. We stayed in touch online and finalized our constitution digitally early in the summer, and the group gained official approval in fall 2018. Finally, the organization was official!

Regular legislative sessions take place each spring in Oklahoma, and the 2019 session was the first with a truly growing "teacher caucus" in the legislature, including one teacher from our local district. This year brought an added $1,200 raise for teachers, plus around $70 million added to the funding formula, which, while welcome, doesn't get us close to the 2008 funding levels for which we had hoped (and our public school budgets in 2008 were hardly lucrative). We do know that this amount plus last year's salary increase did not do enough to stave off the growing shortage of teachers for our schools—3,038 emergency certifications were approved in the 2018–2019 academic year, and the June 2019 numbers were double those from June 2018 (Eger, 2019). (Note: An emergency certification cannot be granted unless a school administrator requests it, having documented that the district is unable to find a certified applicant. The only starting requirement for the would-be teacher is that they hold *any* bachelor's degree along with this emergency credential. The legislature also recently mandated that they have a bit of professional development before their first school year begins, though this will be difficult to enforce since many are hired very close to the school year's start date or even after the school year has begun.)

As we look toward fall, our student organization continues to seek ways to encourage teachers to see advocacy as a normal and natural part of their work lives. Last winter, in response to our desire to increase the comfort of our teacher colleagues and our preservice teachers, we hosted a community-wide advocacy training event, that several area teachers and administrators attended as our guests. Despite a small turnout (due to icy roads and bad weather), a good mix of participants from the university and the community joined our group to learn how to better advocate from a grassroots organization called Together Oklahoma, an offshoot of the nonprofit, nonpartisan think tank, the Oklahoma Policy Institute. Building on that event, the students plan to share what they learned at a "Pizza & Politics" event this coming fall with their fellow preservice teachers and teacher colleagues, teaching them how to craft and share an "elevator pitch" for or against a bill. To plan the event, the students are being strategic: they've asked many questions on and off campus, of staff, faculty, peers in university courses, fellow teachers, and administrators. Using the input they gathered, they plan to work with our college events manager and the faculty/staff advocacy team (Professional Education Advocacy Team: PEAT) on campus to make the event visible and accessible, considering the area district calendar so it will align with a flexible professional day when more teachers could attend.

The student advocacy organization president collaborated with a graphic designer who offered to do a few logo options at no charge. Then members voted to order buttons and stickers with a logo they collaboratively selected to help raise awareness of their organization. They distributed the products at the campus organization fair and offered attendees an opportunity to join the group. They also provided academic advising offices with some of these stickers and buttons to promote their organization. While they are using Facebook, Twitter, and Instagram to promote events as well (even electing a PR/social media officer), they are finding that email is still the best, most direct way to inform their on-campus peers of opportunities. Through direct emails, in addition to posting meeting information on the campus student listserv, they are working hard to spread the word about their work. They've discussed altering the constitution to formally allow alumni membership, but for the short term, they plan to keep alumni in the loop informally, so as to not lose touch with their fellow advocates, some of whom already were teaching nearby and others who are just beginning as teachers in area school districts. Another goal is to raise funds for a teacher advocate award, designed to honor and promote advocates to serve as role models to the preservice teachers whom we want to get more involved.

In the spring semester of 2019, I had bumped into more than one of the group's officers at the capitol. I could not have been more proud to introduce the organization's president, a graduate student and teacher, to my colleagues from around the state. The student organization hosted our area legislators on April 12, 2019, for an education focused Q&A, and the students' questions were respectful but insistent that more must be done. The best part? All three legislators who planned to attend—one senator (who ultimately was not able to make it), and two freshman representatives—are genuine allies in the fight for public education. This year the newly formed faculty/staff advocacy team from our professional education unit collaborated with the student group to schedule and get the word out about the legislator Q&A event. Attendance was fantastic—staff, faculty, and graduate students from across campus showed up to hear the student-led Q&A and visit with policy makers. This event was our greatest success to date, nearly filling a lecture hall that holds 150.

Several things have come to light for me in this year following the walkout. Inviting more preservice teachers and graduate students to the work was far more important for my own morale than I had realized. This fall, I will enter my twentieth year in education, and I don't think I realized how emotionally tired I was in connection with policy advocacy in our state. Not only do I now have a new set of energetic allies at my home institution, I also have the honor and privilege of sharing the work with colleagues from other universities (the Oklahoma Association of Colleges of Teacher Education has really worked hard at collaborative advocacy) and other state agencies. As a former elementary ed/literacy faculty member and curriculum studies scholar, I am thrilled to hear advocacy conversations, finally, naturally spilling over into curricular discussions. What a gift it would be to see this generation of teachers reject the snake oil of scripted curricula and one-size-fits-all programs once and for all and insist on quality teaching for our children. To get there, though, we have to maintain a critical mass of prepared educators who know the work. Addressing the teacher shortage will need to coincide with critical, teacher-led conversations on curriculum that are beginning to take root more deeply.

Oklahomans are known for our resilience. When she was a young woman, my grandmother stayed while the rest of her family left for California. I think about her often when I am frustrated with my state, particularly when I consider that *this* drought was of our own making from far too many years of poor policy and little legislator accountability, both of which have ignored the needs of our children in schools. Fortunately, this is a disaster we can clean up, with persistence rather than with patience. I am relieved to see that teachers' patience has finally run dry; educators—and soon-to-be educators—in Oklahoma continue to, professionally but persistently, demand better. They are getting to know their legislators by inviting them to campus, and they are, increasingly, feeling confident enough to visit the capitol and get to know legislators and their staff. One of my favorite questions from the April 2019 Q&A event is this: "How did you become interested in running for office? What was that process like?" At least one of our student advocates is considering a run for office someday. That's one of the few exits from the classroom for a graduate that I would not mourn. In fact, former educators and other education allies in the legislature have formed a bipartisan, bicameral group calling themselves "edvocates." While they were not granted official status as a caucus, they carry on unofficially, hosting stakeholder events and inviting educators and teacher educators to be part of the conversation, considering solutions to the teacher shortage and ways to better support our public schools. Educators who remain in Oklahoma continue learning how best to prioritize our needs and our children's and teens' needs and how to work together to meet them. A bit more than one year after the walkout, we are better organized and better educated on how to proceed. We are teachers, after all; we keep learning.

What We Noticed as We Read This Chapter

More than any other chapter in this section, Robin Fuxa's narrative weaves together the approaches of everyday advocacy with the kind of "big A" advocacy that focuses legislative action, that is more typically seen in popular media. But rather than simply pontificating on the hows and whys of a particular teacher labor movement in Oklahoma, Robin's chapter contextualizes the moments leading up to the walkout across several dimensions. First, we can read into this chapter the historic efforts—such as the erosion of equity and job security for teachers across the country—that led to this particular movement. Next, she offers a clear-eyed perspective of her own development as a member of the teaching profession and the kinds of advocacy and activism that she has grown into over the years. Finally, by considering these factors, we can read this chapter as an exploration of a once-present moment and the choices, dilemmas, and learning opportunities of the preservice teachers Robin is supporting. These are necessarily layered contexts to the way we read this chapter and they offer important opportunities for reflection for you, the readers. Here's what we noticed:

- *Any advocacy moment comes with a history and a context.* As you consider the advocacy efforts you may be involved in, it's important to think about both the historic and personal factors that shape the effort and your understanding of the effort. Equally important are the salient contextual factors of the current setting in which you are entering or working within. Both help guide our decisions as advocates in practice.

Questions to consider: How might you learn more about the history that underlies the issue at the heart of your advocacy? About the present context?

- *Advocacy is a journey.* We note, with interest, Robin's journey as she works alongside students, pointing to a key core belief of advocacy: We are constantly growing and learning. Throughout this chapter, Fuxa highlights key moments in her own trajectory, and there are powerful moments where we get to witness an alignment of interest between her motivations, her students' enthusiasm, and the broader contexts of organized labor in Oklahoma.

  Questions to consider: What are your own roots in advocacy? Are there incidents or experiences you can point to that inspired your interest? How might those experiences impact your next steps? What are the roots for the preservice and practicing teachers with whom you work?

- *Social change happens over time.* Perhaps most importantly, Robin's narrative does not say she simply toppled the inequities that have wormed their way deep into the teaching profession. No single demonstration will dismantle the insidious factors that have diminished teacher power and capital over the past century. And so, we were wary of the ending of the chapter when Robin first shared it with us. It is hard to imagine neatly wrapped-up conclusions to the ongoing struggles in public education today. And it is in this light that we appreciate how Robin explores the notion of "success" with her students. We are reminded that social movements *move* over time. The steady march forward and our participation in this march are very much lessons that Robin impresses on her students and her readers.

  Questions to consider: How can you help the preservice teachers with whom you work to develop the long-term view (and the patience that it requires) and to continue an advocacy mindset when change doesn't happen immediately? How can we make this work sustainable, as part of the professionalism of teachers and teaching?

References

Eger, A. (2019, June 28). Oklahoma's teacher shortage: 3,038 emergency certifications approved, up 54% in 2018-19. *Tulsa World*. Retrieved from https://www.tulsaworld .com/news/local/ education/oklahoma-s-teacher-shortage-emergency-certifications-approved-up-in/article_bc610345-7213-5293-8a49-7e1311c09cf1.html

Fine, R. (2019, March 6). Report: Despite gains from teacher walkout, Oklahoma school funding is still way down. *Oklahoma Policy Institute*. Retrieved from https://okpolicy .org/report-despite-gains-from-teacher-walkout-oklahoma-school-funding-is-still-way -down/

Oklahoma Policy Institute (2019, May 13). State question 640. *Oklahoma Policy Institute*. Retrieved from https://okpolicy.org/state-question-640/

Perry, G. (2017, May 2). Another year goes by, and Oklahoma still leads the nation for cuts to education. Retrieved from https://okpolicy.org/another-year-goes-oklahoma -still-leads-nation-cuts-education/

Chapter 15

"I Must Be Fearless"

Connecting Teacher Research and Advocacy

Cathy Fleischer

Coauthor of this book Cathy Fleischer invites readers to think about the ways classroom-based research can help educators gain confidence to go public with their own stories of teaching. Sharing experiences from her work with teachers in several settings, she calls for all of us to become knowledgeable and work in smart ways to educate others.

Many years ago, I sat in the audience at a state board of education meeting as the board was considering a new language arts curriculum, a curriculum designed by classroom teachers and that relied on research-based best practices regarding literacy and literacy instruction. (Yes, this *was* many years ago!) As I listened to teacher after teacher stand up to testify about the strength of this curriculum, I was stunned at the state board's disrespect: talking to each other, walking on and off stage, ignoring the teachers' heartfelt words of support.

But all this changed during the section of the meeting reserved for testimony from the public. I watched as a parent stood up to testify—shaking all over but clutching in her hands a pink booklet written by one of the teachers who had testified earlier that morning. The parent spoke haltingly but with passion about the education her child was receiving, peppering her speech with terminology and specific examples of why certain ways of literacy instruction worked well for her child and other children in the class. You could have heard a pin drop in the room, as the board members listened attentively, nodding in agreement, clearly moved by the parent's passion.

The pink booklet that the parent held so tightly was written by her child's first grade teacher, the late Cathy Gwizdala. Cathy G. wrote the book for all the parents of the students she taught, sharing with them the findings of her own classroom research, using samples from student work to demonstrate for them the journey their students would take in learning to read and write in her classroom. This parent—and many others—read the booklet and gained new understandings of how literacy would be taught in the classroom with specific examples that helped that literacy instruction come alive. This parent—so confident in Cathy G.'s explanation—felt confident explaining to the state board why this way of teaching worked. This school board heard the words (literally, the words written by Cathy G.) spoken by the parent in ways they couldn't hear them when they were spoken by the teachers. What a lesson in advocacy that was: the importance of both identifying a decision-maker and discovering whom the decision maker would most listen to!

But there is another lesson in advocacy that shines forth from this moment in time— what it means for teacher advocates to work in ways that are *smart*. Smart advocates, as we explained in Chapter 2, learn the issue at the center of their advocacy deeply: they read the research pertinent to the issue, familiarize themselves with curricular practices connected to that research, and find ways to situate that knowledge within their own classroom instruction. That knowledge lets them speak confidently with others about research-based best practices so that they can advocate for their issue, knowing what they know.

They also, as the pink booklet example above shows, increase their knowledge when they integrate what others have said with what they learn from conducting their own classroom research. When teachers raise questions about their own teaching and learning and then immerse themselves in systematic, structured, and ethical inquiry, they become knowledgeable in new ways and they become confident in sharing their understanding with others (Chiseri-Strater & Sunstein, 2006; Cochran-Smith & Lytle, 2009; Mohr & Maclean, 1999). Like when Gwizdala wrote that booklet for parents, whenever teacher researchers share their learning with administrators, other teachers, or members of the community, they proudly proclaim to others that they are indeed well-informed and insightful—someone to be listened to.

For over 20 years, I have been involved in a teacher research support group that was initially designed to help teachers conduct research into their own classrooms in order to reconsider their own teaching and learning practices. The group meets once a month over wine and pizza as we delve into the questions (what we call *the true wonderings*) each of them has decided to pursue over the year: questions about reading and writing instruction, classroom libraries, assessment, curriculum, and more. The teachers read widely, sharing titles of articles and books that have inspired them, but most importantly, they collect data from their own classrooms through interviews with students and colleagues, copious observation notes, surveys, student artifacts, and more. They bring their data to the meetings, and together we talk through the themes we notice. Over time, they figure out how to go public with their findings, whether that means having a discussion with an administrator, writing a journal article, giving a presentation for colleagues, or developing a handbook for parents.

Recently, now that many of these teachers have gone through everyday advocacy training, we've been able to articulate the connections between teacher research and advocacy more clearly. Teachers in the group have adopted a mantra, the words they say to colleagues and administrators when they want to suggest a different way of thinking about curriculum and pedagogy. "According to my research . . ." they begin, and they then explain how their classroom-based inquiry led them to rethink assessment tools, approaches to reading instruction, or classroom set-up. "According to my research" carries weight, identifying the teacher as a knowledgeable professional who is capable of decision-making and who is willing to help educate others.

How does this connect to everyday advocacy? When teacher researchers gain confidence in their own expertise, they are able to advocate for particular ways of teaching and learning. They are able to explain to others the *whys* and *hows* of their teaching, situating their knowledge in the specifics of their own research project. Teacher research and advocacy, we all have come to realize, are inextricably intertwined.

In Practice: Connecting Teacher Research and Advocacy in a Classroom Setting

Over the years I have tried to pass along to teachers, both in my research group and in the classroom, the lessons I've learned about the connections between teacher research (TR) and advocacy. In methods courses, for example, I always introduce preservice teachers to classroom research, helping them consider how TR can help them speak to administrators and parents with confidence. In networks I cofacilitate for elementary grade teachers, I offer explicit instruction in teacher research and I suggest multiple venues where they could/should share their findings so they can create changes in how literacy education is conceived in their schools. In our local National Writing Project (NWP) Summer Institutes, I share the connections between teacher research and advocacy, urging teachers to use their voices and expertise to effect change.

Last winter I offered a more explicit version of ways to connect TR and advocacy in a course I taught for the coordinators and faculty of Bright Futures, a 21st Century Community Learning Centers after-school program for students in high-needs school districts in southeastern Michigan. The twenty-one Bright Futures teachers and coordinators who signed up for the Winter Writing Institute came to the course for various reasons and with varying needs, each unique to their teaching contexts, but they also brought to the table certain commonalities of context. Housed in 25 schools and steeped in a culture of social emotional learning, the Bright Futures program works most directly with students who come from high-poverty backgrounds and it demonstrates, daily, its commitment to and connections with the students and their families.

The Winter Writing Institute unfolded in many ways like a traditional NWP Summer Institute, as teachers experienced the principles of teacher as writer, teacher as researcher, and teacher as professional and leader. But, given the connections I wanted to promote between teacher research and advocacy, I decided to add a linked yet explicit advocacy component. In their role as *teacher researchers*, they were asked to continue to grow in their knowledge of writing instruction by reading about best practices and considering how those practices might transfer to their own classroom contexts. In this part of the course, the participants identified a research question, based in true wondering, about their teaching of writing, and composed a short, annotated bibliography on that question. They then shifted to creating a teacher research proposal based on their question, the research they had read, and the implications of that research for their own setting. In other words, the goal of this section of the class was to dive into the scholarly and pedagogical conversations in the field of literacy that surrounded their curiosity and to then turn their new knowledge into a specific question they could research in their classroom the following year that would enable them to improve their teaching and their students' learning. Next, in their role as *teacher leader, professional, and advocate*, I asked them to consider their TR proposal, specifically the question and what they had learned thus far about the question, and determine who else needed to know more about it. As I explained in the syllabus:

To help others outside of this group know more about how and why you teach, you will create a plan to help others learn more about the teaching of writing: your audience could be other Bright Futures teachers, it could be parents, it could be members of the community in which you teach and learn.

Participants began their advocacy plans by considering these questions:

- What do others need to understand about writing and the teaching of writing?
- Who in my setting needs to understand this?
- What can I do to help them understand this better?
- How can I make this happen?

Again, the goal of this project was to connect research, specifically teacher research, with advocacy—working in smart ways to learn as much as possible about their research interest so that they could share that knowledge intentionally and convincingly with others.

One participant, for example, created a plan designed to support her research into student voice in writing, explaining, "I feel that parents and school faculty need to better understand that writing and helping students find their voice is one of our key goals. It is up to myself and my staff to make sure we are communicating this to other stakeholders, including those mentioned above and to the Board of Education and community at large." She named specific actions to help others in her school community understand why student voice is so important:

1. Introduce diverse writing strategies to students and share their work with school staff, parents, and other community members.
2. Promote the use of writing with staff members: short writing prompts in staff meetings, create resource folder on Google drive from which staff can investigate resources
3. Plan a family writing night so that parents, siblings, and community members can engage in some of these new and fun strategies

Another participant focused on creativity in writing, explaining, "Adults need to remember the fun of writing and to ensure sacred writing time for students to explore the creativeness of writing. If students are only asked to write academically, or if their creative writing and thoughts are judged and graded, they lose the writing spirit." His actions included:

1. My first step is to start this at my own program! I need to create a space for students to free-write and find a place where their words and voice won't be judged.
2. Starting this spring, I want to create a space dedicated to writing. It will have authors' words on the walls, lamps instead of overhead lights, and an endless supply of paper and pencils.
3. I also want to build up to giving the students time to write. I will start with writing in community building one day a week, and then will grow that to two or three days a week.
4. In the fall, I will start free, creative writing at the beginning of the day, before community building. I will also encourage students to keep reading, and I will keep growing our library.
5. We will have a book club and writing club for students so that they can share their work with others. I will continue to have clubs dedicated to writing: comic book club, script writing, creative writing.
6. I will have a family night where parents can learn about writing for fun and where students can present to their families.
7. I will publish the students' work proudly in a book, so that they know their voice matters.

As I read these excerpts from their proposals (and there are others that are equally interesting), I noticed how these Bright Futures teachers thoughtfully mix teaching and advocacy; teacher research and scholarly research; student work and public outreach. And as they reflected on their experiences, I could see how these connections impacted their next steps in their teaching lives. "As a leader and advocate," one teacher noted, "I must be able to research and share best practices with other educators and youth workers"—demonstrating her understanding of the importance of immersing herself in research-based practices as a first step toward outreach to colleagues. Another teacher focused on the impact of this work on the families, youth, and community: "Our families, youth, and community are depending on the work that we do. If we do not use our voices to advocate for those who have been disempowered, falsely empowered, or brushed to the wayside, we are letting them down." And yet another teacher spoke to the changes in the self that this kind of work requires (and supports): "Because if I really want to be an advocate and a leader, I have to be brave and confident. I must understand that I have a voice and research to share . . . I must be fearless."

Reaching out to others to share our knowledge can be scary. But those teachers who immerse themselves in the power of teacher research (from Cathy Gwizdala to the members of our teacher research group to these Bright Futures teachers) are able to say more confidently, "According to my research . . ." And when they do—when they work in ways that build their knowledge and recognize their own contexts—they can be brave and fearless. And that can be the beginning of change.

What Antero Noticed as He Read This Chapter

Cathy's chapter in this section zooms in on examples of everyday advocacy in action and demonstrates much of the work we've discussed throughout the book so far. We've spent a lot of time talking about our audience and successfully conveying our advocacy issues to individuals in positions of power as well as to colleagues and partners who can collaborate with us on the important work we want to do. The opening of this chapter, however, poses an important consideration: though teachers are often the experts when it comes to powerful literacy instruction and advocacy, perhaps we are not always the best suited for conveying our messages most effectively. As the anecdote of a parent reiterating the words of Cathy Gwizdala to help shift the school board's perspective on literacy reminds us, partners help us consider whose voices are heard and how we can collaboratively work together toward common goals. I notice other advocacy lessons as well.

- *Humility must sit at the core of our work as advocates for the teaching profession.* As much as we hope new teachers (and their teacher educators) complete their teacher education programs with a growing sense of confidence in their skills and expertise, we also caution educators of all ages to carry their hard-earned expertise with a sense of humility alongside that burgeoning confidence. Humility—knowing when to speak up, when to step back, and when to allow other people's expertise to help illuminate the problems of practice at hand—is a fraught concept, often assumed to be an act of meekness or to indicate a lack of confidence. However, as Cathy's chapter highlights, that couldn't be further from the truth: true humility allows us to feel confident in those around us—like the parent invoking the words of Cathy Gwizdala—as equal, or even greater than equal, contributors to a shared sense of literacy focus.

Questions to consider: Where do you see the idea of humility playing out in your own teaching? In your own practice? How might you help the preservice and practicing teachers recognize both its importance and its connection to advocacy?

- *Advocacy is not a hard-won thing that is gained overnight.* Neither is it like the skill of riding a bike, where once you know how to do it, it is ingrained in your muscle memory for life. Instead, advocacy is a kind of practice that must grow over time. Cathy's chapter illustrates the many ways that her understanding of advocacy has changed substantially over the years that she's worked inside classrooms, in National Writing Project summer institutes, and professional development experiences.

  Questions to consider: What is your understanding of advocacy right now? What was it five years ago? How can you imagine it growing over time?

- *How we teach advocacy shifts depending on context and purpose.* The context in which you may be leading courses and disseminating information about advocacy may change from one semester to the next. The second half of Cathy's chapter illustrates how she flexibly navigated the varied settings through which she taught advocacy. As English educators, we can introduce advocacy through undergraduate and graduate classes, workshops, teacher groups, and more.

Questions to consider: In what settings do you work with teachers? How might you introduce advocacy practices in various settings? How might you help teachers build their notion of advocacy over time and in multiple spaces?

Like other chapters in this section, Cathy's chapter helps offer pragmatic language you can adapt in your classes. It also shows how students actually responded to the advocacy prompts. Though we might not think that course work is where students develop a sense of being "brave and fearless," the framing of this chapter illustrates how these feelings are cultivated alongside the sense of humility that teachers like Cathy bring to our work.

References

Chiseri-Strater, E., & Sunstein, B. (2006). *What works? A practical guide for teacher research*. Portsmout, NH: Heinemann.

Cochran-Smith, M., & Lytle, S. (2009). *Inquiry as stance: Practitioner research for the next generation*. New York, NY: Teachers College Press.

Mohr, M., & MacLean, M. S. (1999). *Teacher researchers at work*. Berkeley, CA: National Writing Project.

Conclusion

Expanding the Scope of Everyday Advocacy

Throughout this book we've talked about how to create an advocacy stance among teachers. This book, in other words, is an attempt to advocate *for* advocacy: our contribution to changing the narrative regarding teaching and teacher education toward one that includes advocacy as a pillar of teacher knowledge. And, in case it isn't clear by now, we continually learn and grow our thinking as we sit in dialogue with the many teachers and teacher educators across the country who are doing the complex and humanizing work of advocacy, every day, in their classrooms, in their research, and in the ways they continuously hold up our profession in perpetually perilous times.

We are grateful to be able to share through this book the approaches of some of the teachers who are practicing advocacy in their own settings. Looking at the panoply of voices, we notice how thoughtfully (and distinctly), they are working in ways that are smart (as they learn more about their issue through reading, talking to others, and conducting teacher research), safe (as they develop allies and collaborators both in their setting and beyond), savvy (as they identify audiences for what they've discovered about their issue, frame their issue to reach those audiences, create a strategy for how to proceed, and find just-right tactics to help educate others), and sustainable (as they make advocacy *part* of their lives as teachers, rather than one more add-on). We've also seen how teacher educators are doing this work, introducing preservice teachers and practicing teachers to the idea of advocacy through courses, clubs, and workshops. As we've stated before, we hope these are all examples you can use to push against inertia to create a more equitable instantiation of ELA in your own teaching and learning practice.

As we conclude this book, we want to raise three final questions:

- How do we build a movement of teachers committed to changing the narrative about public education?
- How do we spread the word about the importance of an advocacy stance?
- How do we sustain that work?

As we thought about the last two questions, Cathy kept returning to a poem by Marge Piercy called "The Low Road," a poem that hangs over her desk where she can see it every day. The poem gives a glimpse into what the world could look like if we shift our vision of change-making from a focus on one to a focus on we. Piercy presses us to think about what can happen when we have two, three, four, a dozen, a hundred, a thousand others—all united in a single cause, with the increased power that arises with each expansion. "It goes one at a time," she suggests, but "starts at the moment when you say We." ("The Low Road," Piercy, 1980)

Over the past several years, we have worked with many practicing teachers from rural, urban, and suburban settings and invited them to become part of the *we* and to see themselves as advocating for the students they teach, for the beliefs they hold surrounding literacy education, and for the practices that follow from those beliefs. We've taught graduate level courses (either specifically designed around advocacy or that include an in-depth section about advocacy interwoven into the course); we've led advocacy workshops and presentations of many lengths (from one to three hours long) at local, state, and national conferences; and Cathy has facilitated two- and three-day Everyday Advocacy Summer Institutes. While the approach in each of these settings varies (because of purpose, context, and time constraints), the message across them remains the same: teachers are uniquely situated to share their stories and raise their voices; teachers can learn how to do this in ways that are smart, safe, savvy, and sustainable; teachers can make this a part of their everyday lives.

Years of doing this work with groups of committed and strong teachers in diverse settings has been inspiring: we've watched individuals find new ways to incorporate advocacy into their day-to day teaching lives, from small steps to intricate action plans; we've seen them take on the identity of advocate in their dealings with parents, administrators, colleagues, and the community. Amid our delight at these changes, we keep coming back to the question of how to expand toward the *we* that Marge Piercy calls for. Specifically, how can teacher educators help create a sea change regarding advocacy—from seeing everyday advocacy as a one-teacher-at-a-time kind of work to a more transformative moment that grows the movement exponentially? Knowing that there are many approaches that can be taken toward sustainably invigorating the teaching of ELA with the principles of everyday advocacy, the next few pages outline one approach that Cathy has led alongside teachers.

Advocacy Ambassadors as a Transformative Possibility

As we began floating the idea of broadening engagement with advocacy to colleagues who share our commitments, we came to ask this question: What if we shifted the Everyday Advocacy Summer Institute format of "training" teachers to become individual advocates in their local settings to one that builds on that training to help teachers become ambassadors for this work, challenging them to take on the role of spreading the word of advocacy? In other words, what would happen if we expanded the reach of everyday advocacy by inviting each teacher participant who attended the Institute to create a plan to introduce advocacy to other teachers in their settings?

We hoped that widening the focus of our summer work and the role of the Institute's participants to that of ambassador would increase the *we*, creating an even larger cadre of teachers who considered advocacy part of their normal role as teachers. Think of it this way: When we—any of the thoughtful teacher educators represented in this book—introduce advocacy measures to the preservice or practicing teachers in our classes or workshops, we initiate 15 or 20 or 30 teachers into this world of change-making. When we add to that an ambassador approach, we create the opportunity for that number to expand exponentially: Each of those 15 or 20 or 30 teachers then initiates 15 or 20 or 30 more teachers in their own settings, and so on. Like a pebble thrown in a pond, the way of thinking spreads widely (see Figure C.1).

This idea took form in the summer of 2019, when Cathy received a regional seed grant from the National Writing Project to create a core group of everyday advocacy ambassadors. These ambassadors, all NWP teacher consultants recommended by

Figure C.1 Expanding the Reach of Everyday Advocacy

Figure C.1a

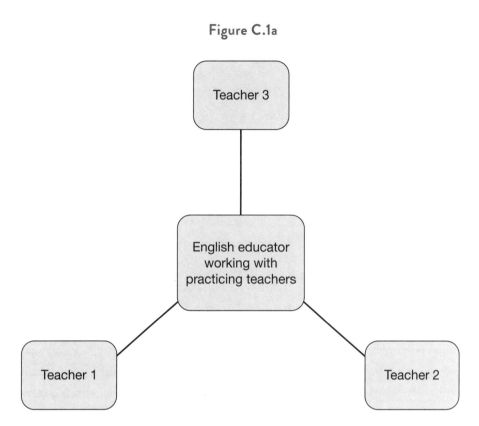

Figure C.1b

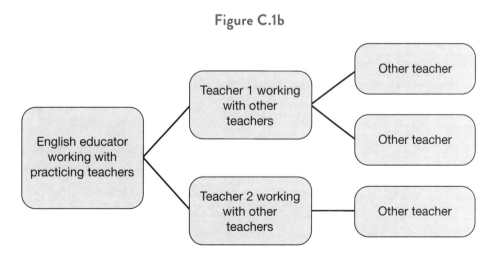

their site directors, traveled to Eastern Michigan University from Michigan and three surrounding states (Wisconsin, Illinois, and Ohio) for a 2-day summer workshop focused on three goals:

1. to learn about the everyday advocacy approach to change-making;
2. to bring this work back to their own NWP sites through workshops, conferences, and other initiatives; and
3. to promote everyday advocacy in their own local, state, and regional settings.

For the first day and a half, Cathy facilitated a version of Everyday Advocacy Summer Institute much as she had done in the past, integrating many of the ideas discussed in Part I of this book and found on the Everyday Advocacy website (https://everydayadvocacy.org/). That is, participants talked about the reasons for seeing advocacy as part of their everyday lives as teachers, even as we—participants and facilitators—identified the roadblocks (both real and perceived) that stand in teachers' ways. We looked together at the three core ideas (storytelling as advocacy, identifying and framing an issue, and taking action), and we wrote and shared our personal stories of teaching with others in order to identify shared values. Participants then named personal issues of concern, situating those concerns within our shared values, and learned how to frame an issue in terms of their identified audience of decision-makers and the values those decision-makers may hold. Together, we thought about how to create allies, messages, and strategies, and we identified tactics that fit individual contexts, purposes, and audiences. Each participant then created an individual action plan for making change in their local setting, focusing on the personal issue they had identified as important for their own context. These individual action plans covered a range of ideas and approaches. Among them were:

- Foster a school-wide reading culture, by helping teachers, administrators make visible their own reading lives;
- Help parents and communities understand the importance of authentic writing experiences and purposes for primary-level writers;
- Shift a school culture to recognize the importance of voice and choice for secondary student writers;

- Convince administrators and parents in a faith-based school about the need for conversations about how young adult literature can serve as both mirrors and windows for students to their shared-faith experience.

We emphasized the importance of working in smart, safe, savvy, and sustainable ways, and we also emphasized that the only way advocacy can become a way of life for teachers (rather than an assignment from an institute or class) is to create systems and supports for this work in the weeks, months, and years after the institute ends.

On the afternoon of the last day, however, we switched gears to consider how each participant could take what they learned back to their own setting to introduce everyday advocacy to other teachers. Keeping in mind the ways of advocacy that we had been learning and working together in teams from each Writing Project site, teachers created locally based plans to expand the reach of this work. We began by thinking about how to create outreach plans that met the needs, values, and beliefs of their particular communities, couching this shift in emphasis on the now-familiar language of working in ways that are smart, safe, savvy, and sustainable. What does it mean for everyday advocacy ambassadors to work in these ways?

When ambassadors work in ways that are smart, they
- Learn more about what everyday advocacy looks like (the information they learned in the first day and a half of the institute and the variety of approaches and the variety of action plans written by their colleagues in the summer institute)
- Increase their knowledge of everyday advocacy by diving even more deeply into the Everyday Advocacy website and other resources
- Learn more about the communities in which they will want to share everyday advocacy ideas: what are their community's needs, values, beliefs?

When ambassadors work in ways that are safe, they
- Find professional learning allies in their setting (other NWP Teacher Consultants, state NWP and NCTE leaders, others) who might share their values and support this work

When ambassadors work in ways that are savvy, they
- Create an action plan (like the plans they created for their own schools) for ways to help other teachers and administrators learn more about everyday advocacy

When ambassadors work in ways that are sustainable, they
- Create a network of others (colleagues in the summer institute) that will support them in continuing the work

We then brainstormed ways they could imagine networking to spread the word and the work. Cathy began with a few starter ideas:

- Create professional learning opportunities through your NWP sites: from one-shot, day-long events to year-long learning communities focused on advocacy training
- Present at state and local conferences about everyday advocacy
- Find support through this group, especially through responses to each other's plans, and have monthly zoom meetings to check progress

The teachers quickly added a host of other ideas to reach colleagues, students, and community members:

- Write an article for our state ELA journals or present at state conferences
- Trade resources and present with other community groups interested in this work
- Partner with college professors doing this work
- Facilitate advocacy workshops for student groups
- Create a summer advocacy writing camp for students
- Share with colleagues in our schools
- Share ideas with union leaders

Next, the budding ambassadors worked with their teams from each represented Writing Project site to create a plan for spreading the work of advocacy. As they began, Cathy asked them to consider the same kinds of questions that informed their approach to their individual advocacy plan: Who is your audience? What professional learning approach will best reach that audience? Who are the decision-makers whose support you will need to work with other teachers? What elevator speech will you make to convince a decision-maker about the importance of this work? What's the timeline?

In a short two-hour period, participants wrote thoughtful starts to their projects (starts that are continuing to take shape in these months after the Institute and supported by colleagues in our monthly Google Hangouts). Several participants chose to introduce their Writing Project colleagues to advocacy through a just-a-taste-of-advocacy event, at which the focus would be on one small portion of the advocacy training."Tastings" were configured differently but all consisted of a portion that participants thought would whet the appetite of their colleagues, raise interest in advocacy, and promote a longer professional learning experience the next summer. Some participants created a plan for outreach to teachers in their own schools, sometimes within an already existing group at the school. One of these plans focused on framing, in hopes of coming up with different and better solutions to the challenges they face. One group focused on the idea of advocacy as storytelling as part of their own Writing Project site's move forward: each Writing Project Teacher Consultant telling their individual story of self within the NWP, looking across those stories for shared values (story of us); and identifying the next steps in rethinking and revitalizing their site (story of now). Still others focused on: adding an everyday advocacy corner in their Writing Project's twice-monthly newsletter; initiating regular Twitter chats and Facebook posts about advocacy, directed at their Writing Project teachers; and presenting at state-wide conferences.

Starting "When You Say *We*": A Call for Advocacy Ambassadors

As the work described above continues to develop, we can already see how more teachers are learning about everyday advocacy. When teachers who are trained in advocacy work intentionally to spread the word of advocacy, they can make exponential change, harkening back to the Marge Piercy poem invoked at the beginning of the chapter. Despite our profession's current overemphasis on licenses, credentials, and documented forms of professional accountability, there is no everyday advocacy arbiter, determining if your efforts are worthy or if they *count*. Rather, if you find yourself committed to the ethos of advocacy that we've outlined throughout this volume and you are invested in shaping the contexts of literacy in your teaching site, you *are* an advocate. In this way, you are also a delegate, representing the demands of advocacy in a shifting and (often) inequitable world. You are, by definition, an ambassador for the more just forms of ELA instruction you uphold. Own this title and live up to it. No matter how different your forms of advocacy and action may look from the voices in this book, together we are a *we* in the very sense that Piercy describes.

Seeking collective action in diverse forms and across myriad contexts, our charge to our fellow teacher educators and teacher leaders is this: how can we simultaneously help the preservice and practicing teachers with whom we work to feel comfortable in the role of advocacy in their own teaching contexts and to consider ways to help other teachers take on that role? In other words, how can we increase the *we* in order to create a culture in which advocacy becomes the norm and teachers teach other teachers how to advocate.

Index

AACTE. *see* American Association of Colleges of Teacher Education (AACTE)

action(s)
  in creating change, 23–29, 24*f*
  writing into, 160–68

action-oriented steps
  described, 10
  in everyday advocacy, 10, 10*f*

action plans
  components of, 30–31
  creating, 29–32, 35–36
  Felik's, 37–39
  strategy of, 30–31

action principles, 24–29, 24*f*
  build awareness, 24*f*, 25
  defined, 24–25
  discover who's in charge, 24*f*, 28
  find allies, 24*f*, 25–26
  identify tactics, 24*f*, 28–29
  stay on point, 24*f*, 26–27
  think long-term, celebrate short-term, 24*f*, 27–28

acts of composing
  advocacy efforts as, 88

Adiche, C.N., 16*n*

advocacy. *see also* everyday advocacy
  as "a practice of passion," 140–47
  celebrate creativity, play, and imagination, 112

composing as teacher–writers, 87–96
  (*see also* composing advocacy)
context and purpose of, 194–95
core ideas surrounding, 12–32
defined, 140–41, 146
empathic listening in, 95
equity in, 95
everyday (*see* everyday advocacy)
finding joy in, 174–75
forms of, 167
framing in, 156–57
going public with, 167
growth and, 97–104
history and context of, 184–85
humility and, 193–94
identity and, 162–63
importance of, 7–39
as journey, 185
learning and, 74
legislative, 9–10, 10*f*
local constituents in, 102
making time and space for, 121–22, 174–75
new vision for, 163–64
as not solo process, 145–46
in online spaces, 140–47 (*see also* advocacy in online spaces)
as part of teacher identity, 158
patience and, 194
personal growth with, 97–104

About the Authors

Cathy Fleischer is a professor of English education at Eastern Michigan University where she co-directs the Eastern Michigan Writing Project. She publishes widely, leads professional learning experiences, and is committed to helping teachers raise their voices to change the public narrative about schooling.

Antero Garcia is an Assistant Professor in the Graduate School of Education at Stanford University. His other books include *Good Reception: Teens, Teachers, and Mobile Media in a Los Angeles High School* and *Pose, Wobble, Flow: A Culturally Proactive Approach to Literacy Instruction*.